115646

D0914188

PRACTICAL HYMNOLOGY

BY

HUBERT McNEILL POTEAT, M.A., PhD.

Professor of Latin, Wake Forest College

AMS PRESS

NEW YORK

PRACTICAL HYMNOLOGY

BY

HUBERT McNEILL POTEAT, M.A., PhD.

Professor of Latin, Wake Forest College

"Let the word of Christ dwell in you richly in all wisdom; teaching and admonishing one another in psalms and hymns and spiritual songs, singing with grace in your hearts to the Lord."

115646

ARTI et VERITATI

BOSTON

RICHARD G. BADGER

THE GORHAM PRESS

1921

Library of Congress Cataloging in Publication Data

Poteat, Hubert McNeill, 1886-1958.
   Practical hymnology.

   Reprint of the 1921 ed. published by R. G. Badger,
Boston.
   Includes index.
   1. Hymns, English—History and criticism.
2. Church music. I. Title.
BV310.P7   1975   264'.2   72-1693
ISBN 0-404-09912-2

Reprinted from the edition of 1921, Boston
First AMS edition published in 1975
Manufactured in the United States of America

AMS PRESS INC.
NEW YORK, N. Y. 10003

PREFACE

IN non-ritualistic churches the participation of the congregation in the service is limited to the singing of the hymns. And yet, this exercise, instead of being universally recognized as of vital importance, and treated accordingly, is permitted, in innumerable churches, to sink into a kind of dull lethargy which invariably succeeds in communicating itself, in greater or less degree, to the whole service. The selections are made from a slender cycle that is traversed again and again, week after week, month after month, year after year, with never an attempt to learn new hymns; the spirit of religious fervor and enthusiasm is quenched by the lazy and indifferent manner in which the songs are sung, and nobody knows or cares enough about it to initiate reforms; the pastor has never taken the trouble to study the history of hymn singing or to investigate the circumstances and incidents that cluster around the composition and use of the great hymns; and the people never receive any instruction or inspiration or assistance to supplement their own negligible knowledge of, and interest in, hymnology. As a result of this inexcusable ignorance, carelessness and laziness, the singing of hymns, in all too many churches, instead of being an act of worship, has degenerated into a mere incident of the service,— holding its place solely because of immemorial custom.

A fruitful soil is thus prepared for the purveyor of the cheap, ragtime "hymn." He glibly informs the music committee (composed usually of business men who would be insulted if one ascribed to them any knowledge whatever of music) that his book will wake the congregation out of the lassitude into which it has sunk; that the perfect panacea for the lack of interest in the singing is bound up within the cheap covers of his "Tinkling Cymbal"; that the proper way to stir the souls of the people is to begin with the feet, which, being galvanized into frantic activity under the spell of sundry jigs, waltzes and jazzes, will speedily communicate their exhilaration upward. He succeeds almost invariably in selling his wares, whereupon he goes his way rejoicing to the next church with a "music committee." Now, the cheap hymn book is *not* a cure for the disease; its adoption simply means the substitution of one malady for another.

The cure, then, must be sought elsewhere. It is to be found in the application of a little earnest consideration and study to the whole question of hymnology. The ignorance and indifference of pastor and people are, as suggested above, very largely responsible for conditions as they exist today. This book is prepared with the very practical purpose of presenting what seem to me the most important phases of the subject,—one of which, as far as I can learn, has not been treated at length before,—in as small a compass as possible, to readers who have neither time nor inclination for exhaustive investigation.

Pardon a personal word: I am neither a professional musician nor a teacher of music. The convictions set forth in this little volume have been formed during a long term of service as director of a volunteer choir. Further, I am not in the pay of any publisher of hymn books, nor do I ever expect to be.

I shall be sorry if certain opinions expressed in the following pages appear to any reader to be harsh; but I shall comfort myself with the reflection that every word was written in an earnest endeavor to check what I believe to be a real evil and to promote a deeper interest in the true worship of God.

H. M. P.

Wake Forest, N. C.,
March 30, 1921.

CONTENTS

CHAPTER I

CHAPTER II

CHAPTER III

PRACTICAL HYMNOLOGY

CHAPTER I

HISTORICAL SKETCH[1]

IN the year 1505 the Bohemian Brethren laid the
foundation stone of modern congregational singing by the publication of a hymn book. These
followers of John Hus paved the way, therefore, for
Martin Luther[2] in Germany and for Calvin in
Switzerland. It must be noted, however, that, while
German Protestants, under Luther's leadership,
developed a real hymnody, English and Scottish
Protestants, following Calvin, adopted the metrical
psalm instead of the hymn. Indeed, in the British
Isles, hymn singing was practically outlawed until
the early part of the eighteenth century. Calvin's

---

[1] For the facts presented in this chapter I am chiefly indebted to Dr. Louis F. Benson, whose book, "The English
Hymn, Its Development and Use" (Geo. H. Doran Co., 1915),
is a treasure-house of inspiration as well as information.

[2] "The Congregational Hymn is . . . distinctly the child of
the Reformation."—Benson, *op. cit.*, p. 20. Luther's Catholic
foes insisted that his hymns were responsible for more deser-
tions from the mother church than his sermons and tracts.

contention was, of course, that nothing whatever should be employed in the service except that which had the express authority of Scripture. Man-made hymns, therefore, must be excluded and only the inspired Psalms of David used in worship. This point of view held firm in certain denominational circles until the beginning of the nineteenth century, and proved the most serious obstacle which hymn singing was called upon to face.

The first English hymn book, Myles Coverdale's "Goostly Psalms and Spirituall Songes drawen out of the holy Scripture", published in 1531, was a dull and uninspired attempt to carry forward the Lutheran ideas of hymn singing as against Calvinistic psalmody. In 1546 the King put this production in the *index expurgatorius*, and psalm singing, with the highest official approval, entered upon its two hundred years' career. It must not be understood that hymn singing was absolutely eschewed during this period. On the contrary, sentiment in its favor developed more or less steadily and grew largely out of an ever-increasing dissatisfaction with psalmody. As will be readily seen, the Psalms of David could not possibly give expression to all the thoughts and feelings arising in the minds and hearts of the members of a New Testament church. And so we have, first, a gradual alteration of psalmody—in the hymn direction. Freer paraphrases were used, instead of the former literal translations; other parts of Scripture found their way into the psalm book; then, verses in imitation, or as exposition, of Scripture passages were included; and, finally, we have genuine hymns suggested by Scripture. This evolution proceeded, it may be said, along three lines. There was, first, an effort to improve the literary character of the Psalms. Second, worshipers felt the need of selections which could express more completely their Christian emotions.—In 1679, John Patrick, of London, published "A Century of Select Psalms and portions of the Psalms of David, especially those of praise." Dr. Isaac Watts remarked, some forty years later, that "he hath made use of the present language of Christianity in several Psalms, and left out many of the Judaisms". Patrick was, indeed, Watts' predecessor in this method of adapting the Psalms to current needs,—as Watts freely admitted.—Third, other parts of the Bible began to be paraphrased. As early as 1553 we find "The Actes of the Apostles, translated into Englyshe metre, and dedicated to the Kynges most excellent Maiestye, by Christopher Tye, Doctor in Musyke . . . with notes to eche chapter, to synge and also to play upon the Lute".

William Barton published in 1659 "A Century of Select Hymns", in the preface of which he took an uncompromising stand for hymns. His work may be said to occupy the transition point between the psalm and the hymn, and his influence upon the future progress of hymn singing in England was wide and important.

From 1660 to 1707, the date of the publication of Dr. Watts' "Hymns and Spiritual Songs", we find numerous writers of hymns, all of whom contributed more or less largely to the development of that type of the English hymn which reached its fruition under Watts' inspiration and guidance.

Each division of Nonconformists, of course, met and handled the question of hymns in its own way. Considerations of space make it impossible to discuss the progress of hymn singing in these various denominations. A bit of Baptist history may be presented as fairly typical.

In the year 1606 one John Smyth led his congregation of General, or Arminian, Baptists in a flight to Amsterdam. Smyth believed that the New Covenant was spiritual, proceeding out of the heart, and that, therefore, reading out of a book was no part of spiritual worship, but was the invention of sinful man. "We hold", said he, "that seeing singing a psalm is a part of spiritual worship, it is unlawful to have the book before the eye in time of singing a psalm." The inevitable result of this interesting view was, of course, the custom of singing individually and extemporaneously, as the Spirit gave them utterance. We learn from a book published in London in 1645 that this was, indeed, the type of singing practised in Smyth's church.

In 1678 Thomas Grantham, the official spokesman of the General Baptists in England, delivered himself of a pronouncement to the effect that the New Testament recognized no "promiscuous singing", and no singing by the rules of art, but only the "utterance of psalms and hymns sung by such as God hath fitted thereto by the help of his Spirit for the edification of the listening Church". "If all sing", he proceeded, "there are none to be edified". He insisted, further, that the employment of pleasant tunes would bring back music and instruments, while, if other men's words were used, the way would be open to the similar use of set forms of prayer.

In 1689 the General Baptist Assembly, learning that a few congregations were engaging in the nefarious practice of "promiscuous singing", called upon these erring brethren to show "what psalms they made use of for the matter, and what rules they did settle upon for the manner". The committee of investigation made the following report: "Not the metres composed by Messrs. Sternhold and Hopkins,[3] but a book of metres composed by one

[3] "The whole Booke of Psalmes, collected into Englysh metre by T. Starnhold, I. Hopkins and others"; 1562. This psalter is usually referred to as the "Old Version."

Mr. Barton,[4] and the rules produced to sing these
songs as set down *secundum artem;* viz., as the
musicians do sing according to their gamut,—Sol,
fa, la, my, ray, etc., etc.; which appeared so strange-
ly foreign to the evangelical worship that it was not
conceived anywise safe for the churches to admit
such carnal formalities; but to rest satisfied in this,
till we can see something more perfect in this case,
that as prayer of one in the church is the prayer
of the whole, as a church, so the singing of one
in the church is the singing of the whole church;
and as he that prayeth in the church is to perform
the service as of the ability which God giveth,
even so, he that singeth praises in the church ought
to perform that service as of the ability received
of God; that as a mournful voice becomes the duty
of prayer, so a joyful voice, with gravity, becomes the duty of praising God with a song in the
Church of God". This remarkable judgment was approved by the Assembly, and the practice of "promiscuous singing" among General Baptists was very
limited until the middle of the eighteenth century.
In 1733 there was a wail from Northamptonshire
that some of the churches "had fallen into the way
of singing the Psalms of David, or other men's com-
posures, with tunable notes and a mixed multitude;
which way of singing appears to us wholly unwar-

[4] See pp. 15-16.

rantable from the word of God". But by this time
the Assembly had so far changed its attitude as to
decline to reopen the question.

It will be interesting to note, in passing, two
contemporary Quaker expressions [5] upon the subject of "conjoint singing". George Fox wrote in
his "Journal" in 1655 the following: "Tho: Holme
& Eliz: Holme: att a meetinge in Underbarrow:
were much exercised by ye power of ye Lorde in
songes and Hymns & made melody & rejoyced: &
ye life was raised thereby & refreshed in many: in
ye meetinge". In 1675 the Yearly Meeting officially
declared that "serious sighing, sencible groaning and
reverent singing" were recognized as divers opera-
tions of the Spirit and power of God, and were not
to be discouraged, unless immoderate. All this, of
course, refers to extemporaneous solo performances.
"Conjoint singing" has been introduced into the
Quaker meeting only within the last fifty years,
and is still not practised universally.

Let us now consider briefly the Particular, or
Calvinistic, Baptists. Although their general point
of view was exactly opposite that of the Arminian
branch of the Church, yet some congregations were
unalterably opposed to general participation in
hymn singing. The father of Baptist hymnody was
Benjamin Keach, who printed two collections of

[5] Quoted by Benson, *op. cit.,* p. 95.

hymns; the first, in 1676; the second, in 1691. A bitter controversy was begun in 1690 by a certain Isaac Marlow, a dissenter in Keach's own congregation. This controversy raged for several years and enlisted the energies of many writers on both sides of the question at issue. But after the dust of the conflict had cleared away, Keach's foundation stones were found to be unmoved. A beginning of Baptist hymnody had been made.

Before we pass to the chief figure in the history of hymnology, let us observe the general situation in Nonconformist churches. Psalms were still used exclusively in the majority of these bodies,—lined out by the precentor and droned over by the congregation. Dr. Watts remarked, in the preface to his "Psalms of David Imitated" (1719), that each note was dwelt upon so long as to put "the congregation quite out of breath in singing five or six stanzas". The people knew little about music and cared less. They carried no psalm book to church, but depended upon the clearness of the precentor's enunciation for their words. Watts sums up the situation characteristically in the preface to his "Hymns" of 1707: "While we sing the praises of our God in his Church, we are employ'd in that part of worship which of all others is the nearest a-kin to Heaven; and 'tis pity that this of all others should be perform'd the worst upon Earth. . . . To see the dull Indifference, the negligent and the thoughtless Air that sits upon the Faces of a whole Assembly while the Psalm is on their Lips, might tempt even a charitable Observer to suspect the Fervency of inward Religion, and 'tis much to be fear'd that the minds of most of the Worshippers are absent or unconcern'd. . . . Of all our Religious Solemnities *Psalmodie* is the most unhappily manag'd. That very Action which should elevate us to the most delightful and divine Sensations doth not only flat our Devotion, but too often awakens our Regret, and touches all the Springs of Uneasiness within us".

We pass now to a brief consideration of the work and influence of Isaac Watts [6] (1674-1748). Another quotation from the preface to his "Hymns" (cited above) will be inserted here, because it sets forth with such lucidity and energy the good doctor's view of the malady he proposed to treat. Says he: "I have been long convinc'd, that one great Occasion of this Evil arises from the Matter and Words to which we confine all our Songs. Some of 'em

[6] Among his most familiar hymns are the following: "Come, we that love the Lord"; "High in the Heavens, eternal God"; "How did my heart rejoice to hear"; "Great God, how infinite Thou art"; "O God, our help in ages past"; "Begin, my tongue, some heavenly theme"; "Joy to the world, the Lord is come"; "Alas! and did my Saviour bleed"; "When I survey the wondrous Cross"; "Come, let us join our cheerful songs"; "Come, Holy Spirit, Heavenly Dove"; "Not all the blood of beasts"; "When I can read my title clear"; "Am I a soldier of the Cross"; "Jesus shall reign where'er the sun"; "There is a land of pure delight"; "God is the refuge of His saints."

are almost opposite to the Spirit of the Gospel: Many of them foreign to the State of the New Testament, and widely different from the present Circumstances of Christians. Hence it comes to pass that when spiritual Affections are excited within us, and our Souls are raised a little above this Earth in the beginning of a Psalm, we are check'd on a sudden in our Ascent toward Heaven by some Expressions that are more suited to the Days of *Carnal Ordinances*, and fit only to be sung in the *Worldly Sanctuary*. When we are just entring into an Evangelic Frame by some of the Glories of the Gospel presented in the brightest Figures of *Judaism*, yet the very next line perhaps which the Clerk parcels out unto us, hath something in it so extremely *Jewish* and cloudy, that darkens our Sight of God the Saviour: Thus by keeping too close to *David* in the House of God, the Vail of *Moses* is thrown over our Hearts. While we are kindling into divine Love by the Meditations of the *loving Kindness of God and the Multitude of his tender Mercies*, within a few Verses some dreadful Curse against Men is propos'd to our Lips. . . . Some Sentences of the *Psalmist* that are expressive of the Temper of our own Hearts and the Circumstances of our Lives may Compose our Spirits to Seriousness, and allure us to a sweet Retirement within our selves; but we meet with a following Line which so peculiar-

ly belongs but to one Action or Hour of the Life
of *David* or *Asaph*, that breaks off our Song in the
midst; our Consciences are affrighted lest we should
speak a Falsehood unto God".

Dr. Watts contemplated, and actually submitted
to the Nonconformist public, what was in effect
a new system of church song. He insisted, first,
that the psalmody should be evangelical; second,
that it should be freely composed (that is, that
there should not be too strict adherence to the letter of Scripture); third, that it should express the
thoughts and feelings of the singers, and not of
David or Asaph. His theory of worship embraced
both psalms and hymns, but his views on the proper
use of psalms were somewhat revolutionary. He
maintained that the Psalms, as such, were meant
to be read, and that they ought to be translated
literally. Those church members who declined to
give up psalm singing must use a prose translation,
and so must either master Hebrew music or learn
to chant. To the average Nonconformist, this, of
course, was practically equivalent to the casting
aside of the psalm.

Dr. Watts announced, further, that congregational si ging should not represent God's word to us,
but our word to God. The adoption of this view
made it necessary to omit a number of time-honored
passages of the Psalms, and also compelled some
adaptation of the rest, to the end that David might

speak as he would have spoken, had he been a Christian, an Englishman, and a contemporary of Dr. Watts! Thus, in his "Short Essay toward the Improvement of Psalmody" (1707), Watts remarks: "Judah and Israel may be called England and Scotland, and the land of Canaan may be translated into Great Britain".

In this same essay he set forth his arguments [7] for hymns—"Spiritual Songs of a more evangelic frame for the Use of Divine Worship under the Gospel". They are as follows:

First. A Psalm properly translated for Christian use is no longer inspired as to form and language: only its materials are borrowed from God's Word. It is just as lawful to use other Scriptural thoughts, and compose them into a spiritual song.

Second. The very ends and designs of Psalmody demand songs that shall respond to the fullness of God's revelation of Himself. God's revelation in Christ, and our own devotions responding to it, require Gospel songs.

Third. The Scriptures themselves, especially Eph: v, 19-20, and Col. iii, 16-17, command us to sing and give thanks in the name of Christ. Why shall we pray and preach in that name, and sing under terms of the Law?

Fourth. The Book of Psalms does not provide

[7] Cited by Benson, *op. cit.,* pp. 112-113.

for all occasions of Christian praise, or express all Christian experiences.

Fifth. The primitive "Gifts of the Spirit" covered alike preaching, prayer and song. It is admitted by all that, under the present administration of Grace, ministers are by study and diligence to acquire and cultivate gifts of preaching and prayer. Why shall they not also seek to acquire and cultivate the capacity of composing spiritual songs, and exercise it along with the other parts of worship, preaching and prayer?

Watts began writing hymns as early as 1700, when he was only twenty-five years old. There is a story, fairly well vouched for, to the effect that the young man one day expressed to his father his disgust at the hymns sung in their little meeting-house. The elder Watts invited his son to write some better ones, which Isaac proceeded to do with great alacrity. The congregation liked them and demanded more. The first collection was published under the following impressive title: "Horae Lyricae: Poems, chiefly of the lyric Kind. In two books. I. Songs, etc. sacred to Devotion. II. Odes, Elegys, etc. to Vertue Loyalty and Friendship. By I. Watts. London, printed by S. and D. Bridge, for John Lawrence, at the Sign of the Angel in the Poultrey. MDCCVI". This book was addressed to lovers of poetry, and the few hymns included in it were apparently carefully selected for their distinct literary quality. Watts insisted frequently that his hymns were composed for the plain people and were written in a style which made them easily apprehended by the unpoetic mind. The hymns, therefore, with a literary "taint" he published in his "Horae Lyricae", as noted above, while his simpler songs were issued in 1707 as "Hymns and Spiritual Songs. In Three Books. I. Collected from the Scriptures. II. Compos'd on Divine subjects. III. Prepared for the Lord's Supper. With an Essay towards the improvement of Christian Psalmody, by the use of evangelical Hymns in worship, as well as the Psalms of David. By I. Watts. London, printed by J. Humfreys, for John Lawrence, at the Angel in the Poultrey, 1707". Two years later a second edition of this truly epoch-making publication appeared, containing one hundred and forty-five additional hymns. In 1719 Watts published his "Psalms of David imitated in the language of the New Testament, and Apply'd to the Christian state and worship". This book gave concrete expression to its author's views of psalm singing, mentioned above (pp. 24-25). It contained versions of one hundred and thirty-eight Psalms. His system of praise was now complete, although a number of new hymns appeared in subsequent years.

There is not space to discuss in detail Watts' influence upon the various denominations in England and America. Suffice it to say that his work gave a tremendous impetus to the movement for hymn singing in every Nonconformist body. Numerous so-called supplements were published. For example, "A collection of Hymns from various authors, designed as a Supplement to Dr. Watts's Psalms and Hymns", George Burder, 1784. This was only one of a veritable deluge of such books,—a deluge which flooded England, and, to some extent, New England, until the inevitable reaction began, about the middle of the nineteenth century.

Let us note at this point Watts' influence upon Baptist worship. The General Baptists resisted the onward march of congregational song until the latter half of the eighteenth century. Their first hymnal was issued in 1772 ("Hymns and Spiritual Songs, mostly collected from various authors; with a few that have not been published before"). Two influences contributed to the development of a demand for a hymn book in this branch of the Baptist Church: first, the work of Dr. Watts; and second, the Methodist revival under the Wesleys, which brought into the Baptist fold a great number of new and very enthusiastic converts, in whose souls the stirring evangelistic hymns of the revival still reëchoed. And so, following the "Hymns and Spiritual Songs" of 1772, there appeared in 1785 another

collection by Samuel Deacon, a village clockmaker
—and pastor; and in 1791 the General Baptist Association authorized the publication of yet another,
which entered the field in 1793. Deacon followed with
his "New and large collection of Hymns and Psalms"
(1800). This book was so popular that in 1830
it was revised by a committee of the Association
and adopted as the official General Baptist hymnal.

Among Particular, or Calvinistic, Baptists,
Watts' "Psalms" and "Hymns" attained a wide popularity and exerted a lasting influence. In fact, the
extensive use of his hymns was largely responsible for
what Benson calls "homiletical hymnody", that is,
the practice of selecting the last hymn in the service
for its bearing upon the sermon. This practice,
begun by the Particular Baptists in the middle of
the eighteenth century, has never been dropped in
Baptist churches, and is a distinguishing characteristic which marks the progress of the denomination
in hymnology at every step of the way. The necessity, felt so strongly by ministers, of obtaining
hymns appropriate to their discourses led, from
that time on, to the publication of many new collections and original hymns. Perhaps the most
widely used book was Rippon's "A Selection of
Hymns from the best authors, intended to be an
Appendix to Dr. Watts's Psalms and Hymns"
(London, 1787). This volume, with Watts'

"Psalms" [8] and "Hymns" [9] might almost be regarded as the authorized hymnal of Particular Baptists, since for nearly a hundred years it remained the standard of Baptist hymnody.[10]

In this country, during the early years of the eighteenth century, congregational singing was a dismal business, indeed, if we may accept as true some remarks [11] published in 1720 by a Mr. Symmes, of Boston. He declared that conditions were "indecent," and that, from a lack of books and the inability of the people to sing by note, a very few tunes were sung from memory, "tortured and twisted as every unskillful throat saw fit". Watts' "Psalms Imitated" was first reprinted in America in 1729, by Benjamin Franklin, in Philadelphia. Ten years later the "Hymns" was reprinted in Boston. It is important to note that the revival movement led by the Wesleys and Whitefield was largely instrumental in weaning congregations away from the old "Bay Psalm Book" and in introducing Watts (who, it may be said, did not attain wide popularity until after the Revolution).

Among Baptists, where "promiscuous singing" was practised at all, the "Bay Psalm Book" (1640) had been used. Watts' influence was slower in mak-

---

[8] *Cf.* p. 26.
[9] *Cf.* p. 26.
[10] Benson, *op. cit.*, p. 145, quotes Spurgeon, to the effect that Rippon, with Watts, was used in his Tabernacle until 1866.
[11] *Ibid.*, p. 161.

ing itself felt generally in that denomination than
in any other. One reason for this was that Baptists
rather insisted, from the very first, upon a strictly
denominational hymnody, especially with a view to a
sufficient selection of songs appropriate to the
baptismal service. The first American Baptist
hymnal, "Hymns and Spiritual Songs, collected from
the works of several authors" (Newport, 1766),
opens with sixteen hymns on baptism.

Benson says (p. 199): "The independent and
individualistic spirit combined with denominational
insistence, that has always characterized Baptists,
developed and has maintained a striking proclivity
toward the multiplication of hymn books." And
so we find hymnal after hymnal published during the
years following the appearance of the Newport
book. The large number of these productions ob-
scures, in some measure, the actual development of
the Watts' influence.

Another reason for the tardy reception accorded
to Watts' books by Baptists was that large numbers
of them preferred songs of a somewhat lower literary
grade. This is sad, but true. And unfortunately
that lack of taste and appreciation has perpetuated
itself,—has grown and multiplied,—and furnishes
today a gaping, unappeasable maw, down which flow
successive editions of popular ragtime books, made
over and refurbished from time to time to titillate

anew palates soon satiated with their jingling mediocrity. Early Baptists delighted in highly emotional songs with a rousing chorus, and so a number of books appeared to meet this demand, while Watts took second place. Dr. Benson (pp. 202-203) may be quoted again at this point: "We may judge existing conditions by the character of some of the 170 songs appended to Parkinson's *Selection*.[12] . . . In the first Newton's unfortunate lines are altered to serve as a refrain after each stanza:—

> 'Then be entreated now to stop
> For unless you warning take,
> Ere you are aware you'll drop
> Into the burning lake.'

The third is 'A Dream' of Judgment Day. The fifth is entitled 'Miss Hataway's Experience' and includes her conversation with 'an uncle from whom she had large expectations'. The fifteenth begins, 'Ye scarlet-colour'd sinners, come.'"

And yet, a number of congregations in this country, especially in the North and East, had used Watts' "Psalms" and "Hymns" steadily for a number of years, and their example was wholesome. There was, eventually, a sort of general effort to assemble the best of Baptist hymnody, together with selections from Watts. In 1819 James M. Winchell,

[12] 1809.

of Boston, published "An arrangement of the Psalms, Hymns, and Spiritual Songs . . . of Watts, to which are added, indexes . . . to facilitate the use of the whole". With this was bound up "A Selection of more than 300 Hymns, from the most approved authors".

American Presbyterians for a long time sang psalms exclusively. Most of them were Scotch-Irish who had been raised on psalms and were blissfully ignorant of the existence of Isaac Watts. The few who did know of his work hated him cordially as a presumptuous innovator. And so it is not surprising to find that when the Church divided, in 1741, into the "Old Side" and "New Side," the attempted introduction of Watts' "Psalms Imitated" was one of the causes of the split. In spite of official thunderings, this version of the Psalms steadily increased in popularity, and, before many years had passed, Watts' "Hymns", too, began to be used in Presbyterian churches. Various Synods were called upon to settle the question, but they preferred to leave it to the local churches. There can be no doubt that great impetus was given to hymn singing by the doleful and woebegone manner in which psalms were rendered in the majority of churches. John Adams, after attending a meeting of the "Old Presbyterian Society" in New York in 1774, remarked [13] that

---

[13] Benson, *op. cit.*, p. 184.

their psalmody was "in the *old way*, as we call it—
all the drawling, quavering, discord in the world".
But the Scotch-Irish, particularly in the South,
clung to their Rous' version of the Psalms (1650)
with such tenacity that the mere mention of Watts
was quite sufficient to charge the atmosphere with
electricity. Barlow's revised edition of Watts (1785)
received official approval two years later, but the
powers declined again to say whether they preferred
Watts' hymns or Rous' psalms. And so began the
great "Psalmody Controversy", which continued for
several years with a bitter ferocity difficult for us
in these days to understand. Ministers were driven
from their pulpits; worship was interrupted by
hisses, catcalls and jeers; men went up and down the
land howling imprecations at their brethren of the
opposite party; churches split into factions, battling
with all the holy zeal of crusaders, and finally estab-
lishing two churches where one had existed before.
Although this most unfortunate and disastrous controversy raged parochially for four or five years in
different parts of the country, it was theoretically
settled in 1788 by the adoption of the new "Directory
for the worship of God, of the Presbyterian Church
in the United States of America". Now, this Directory referred to "the duty of Christians to praise
God publiquely by singing psalms or hymns", and
advised, further, that churches should give up the

old custom of "lining out" and devote more time and study to music in the sanctuary. That advice, acted upon generally with considerable enthusiasm, meant, of course, the ultimate triumph of the hymn, that is to say, of Watts. And so "instructors of psalmody" appeared everywhere, classes were organized, and new hymnals published. But "Barlow's Watts" remained for many years the praise book of the large majority of Presbyterian churches.

We may now attempt to summarize Watts' influence. A great many writers have called him the inventor of the vernacular hymn. This is hardly a correct judgment. Watts, rather, established a definite and permanent type of hymn, founded, not on poetic flights or niceties of style, but on the rock-bottom of the emotions and aspirations of the great body of Christians. Dr. Benson's estimate [14] is so clear and forceful that it may be quoted at some length: " . . . he could bring to bear upon his hymn writing a discernment, and a combination of resources, spiritual, intellectual, poetic, utilitarian, possessed by none of his predecessors or all of them if put together. He was not alone in perceiving that an acceptable evangelical Church Song was a spiritual need of his time, but he had the ability to foresee, as other men could not, the possibilities and limitations of the Congregational Hymn in

[14] *Op. cit.,* pp. 206-207.

filling that need. With great assiduity he dedicated his ample gifts to the embodiment of what he saw. He produced a whole cycle of religious song which his own ardent faith made devotional, which his manly and lucid mind made simple and strong, which his poetic feeling and craftmanship made rythmical and often lyrical, and which his sympathy with the people made hymnic. Probably the whole body of his work appealed alike to the people of his time, whose spiritual needs he so clearly apprehended. The larger part of his work proved to be an abiding enrichment of Church Song, and to many its only adequate expression. His best hymns remain permanently, after the winnowing of two centuries, among the classics of devotion".

Watts founded, unconsciously, of course, a school of hymn writers, not all of whom reflected credit on their founder. But in the closing years of the eighteenth century there was a really significant group of Baptist hymn writers of the "School of Watts". Miss Anne Steele [15] was one of this school; others were Benjamin Beddome,[16] Samuel Stennett,[17] and John Fawcett.[18]

[15] Author of "Father of Mercies, in Thy Word"; "He lives, the great Redeemer lives"; "Dear Refuge of my weary soul"; "Father, whate'er of earthly bliss."

[16] Author of "God, in the gospel of His Son."

[17] Author of "Come, every pious heart"; "Majestic sweetness sits enthroned."

[18] Author of "Lord, dismiss us with thy blessing"; "How precious is the Book divine"; "Blest be the tie that binds."

After all, Dr. Watts' greatest achievement was the impetus he gave to actual hymn singing. His hymns were not hung up on the wall as models of devotional poetry; they were *sung*, and sung almost universally. And his success differed from that of the Wesleys, whom we shall study next, in that while they depended largely upon the enthusiasm of a great revival to stimulate interest in their hymns and the singing of them, Watts went to work soberly and seriously, and succeeded magnificently, solely on the merit of his hymns. His "movement" was not revivalistic, but purely liturgical,—"a . . . deliberate undertaking for the 'Renovation of Psalmody' in the ordinary worship of the Church".[19]

We pass now to the great revival under the Wesleys, which occupied the period from 1721 to 1738. It may be repeated that the keynote of Wesleyan hymnody was fervor and enthusiasm, as distinguished from the more sober devoutness of Dr. Watts' work.[20] The history of the missionary activities of John and Charles Wesley in the Colonies is well known. It is of interest to note that John Wesley's first hymn book, "Collection of Psalms and Hymns", was published at Charleston, S. C., in 1737. The following year, on his return to England, he issued

[19] Benson, *op. cit.*, p. 218.
[20] "[Charles] Wesley as a poet is less of a pedagogue and more of a true singer."—Waldo S. Pratt, "Musical Ministries in the Church" (G. Schirmer, New York, 1915), p. 173.

a second volume. Both of these books were sent forth anonymously. A third, appearing in 1739, and bearing the names of both brothers, was one of the first results of the profound evangelical awakening which these remarkable men experienced shortly after their arrival in England from the Colonies. The hymns in this volume proclaimed in clarion tones the deep religious enthusiasm of the authors, and set permanently the style for Methodist hymnody.

Let us consider now their part in the development of the English hymn. In the first place, they were responsible for a great enrichment of the stores of hymns. Their poetical publications covered a period of fifty-three years and numbered fifty-six, of which thirty or more were exclusively original. The whole body of Wesleyan hymns [21] was published in 1872 and filled thirteen volumes (6000 pages).

Secondly, the work of the Wesleys tended to

---

[21] The hymns composed by Charles Wesley have enjoyed a far wider popularity than those of his brother, whose contributions to hymnody were translations from the German. The following may be mentioned: "Ye servants of God, your Master proclaim"; "Come, Thou Almighty King"; "Hark! the herald Angels sing"; "Christ the Lord is risen today"; "Lo! He comes, with clouds descending"; "I know that my Redeemer lives"; "Blow ye the trumpet, blow"; "Sinners turn, why will ye die"; "Jesus, lover of my soul"; "Depth of mercy, can there be"; "A charge to keep I have"; "O for a heart to praise my God"; "Love divine, all loves excelling"; "O for a thousand tongues to sing"; "Our Lord is risen from the dead."

change the ideal of the hymn, both on its spiritual and literary side, and to establish new types of hymns. There was a different atmosphere, a heightening of emotion, a novelty of theme, a new manner of expression. The evangelistic note was strongly stressed, the predominating theme became that of Christian experience, and, finally, there was set a new and higher literary standard. Watts had insisted that the hymn must be kept outside the realm of poetry. The Wesleys, on the other hand, held that a hymn should be a religious lyric; that the people must be lifted to its level and made to feel its beauty. A passage [22] from John Wesley's "Collection" of 1780 may be quoted at this point: "May I be permitted to add a few words with regard to the poetry? . . . In these Hymns there is no doggerel, no botches, nothing put in to patch up the rhyme, no feeble expletives. Here is nothing turgid or bombast on the one hand, or low and creeping on the other. . . . Here are (allow me to say) both the purity, the strength and the elegance of the ENGLISH language: and at the same time the utmost simplicity and plainness, suited to every capacity. Lastly, I desire men of taste to judge (these are the only competent judges;) whether there is not in some of the following verses, the true Spirit of Poetry: such as cannot be acquired by art and

[22] Benson, *op. cit.*, p. 253.

labour; but must be the gift of nature. By labour a man may become a tolerable imitator of SPENSER, SHAKESPEARE, or MILTON, and may heap together pretty compound epithets, as PALE-EYED, WEAK-EYED, and the like. But unless he is born a Poet, he will never attain the genuine SPIRIT OF POETRY." "In the judgment of a recent historian of English Poetry [W. J. Courthope], Wesley 'was fully justified' in making this boast, and his brother Charles was 'the most admirable *devotional* lyric poet in the English language.' " [23]

It must be said, finally, that Wesleyan hymnody made nothing like so wide an extra-denominational appeal as did the productions of Dr. Watts. In the first place, it was far above the spiritual level of the average man; secondly, its theology was denominational and at times aggressively controversial; thirdly, while Watts was universally respected, by Churchmen and Dissenters alike, the Wesleys were regarded outside their own circle as religious cranks: they belonged to "the people called Methodists." As a result of these things, Wesleyan hymns found their way slowly and with difficulty into general popularity and esteem.

In America a great revival flamed out in 1800, one feature of which was the camp meeting. Al-

[23] Benson, *op. cit.*, p. 253.

though this revival began under Presbyterian auspices, Methodists were not long in gaining practical
control of it, partly because the Presbyterian clergy
of the State (Kentucky) held aloof. But a historian [24] of 1847 insists that the Methodist pre-
dominance was gained largely through hymns and
enthusiastic singing. Before the meeting had well
started, the fervor of the people grew so intense that
spontaneous song began to be a feature of the services. A brother or sister, under stress of deep spiritual emotion, would arise and sing extemporaneously, composing words out of Scripture or every-
day speech, and interlarding the performance with
frequent Selahs! and Hallelujahs! And so in this
meeting a new type of hymn was developed, under
Methodist auspices,—the Camp Meeting Hymn. It
deals with the rescue of the sinner from hell fire, it
exhorts the backslider, it paints luridly the flames
of Tophet, it dazzles crudely with attempts to de-
scribe the glory of heaven. Numbers of hymns of
this character have come down to us, and some are
still used in our churches. There is no doubt that
many of them are to be found among the negro
"spirituals,"—more or less altered, of course,—but
still preserving the distinguishing traits of their
nativity.[25]

---

[24] Robert Davidson, quoted by Benson, *op. cit.*, p. 292.
[25] For the words of one of these songs, see p. 68.

As the camp meeting gave way to the more formal and decorous protracted meeting and summer assembly, these crude hymns were displaced by the "Gospel Hymn," associated intimately with the names of Dwight L. Moody and Ira D. Sankey.[26] "For under any circumstances the love of 'popular' song abides. The same streak in human nature that delights in the strains of the music hall demands the 'spiritual song' of the same type. And possibly an element that conscientiously flees the associations of the music hall is the most insistent upon a compensatory light music in the Sunday school and the church." [27]

We pass now to consider the Evangelical Revival under George Whitefield. In 1741 Whitefield and the Wesleys had a sharp doctrinal disagreement, and parted company. The former sprang into prominence at once as a leader on the Calvinistic side; but, while he was a man of wonderful personality, he lacked the Wesleys' ability for organization and sought merely to preach the Gospel. The evangelical revival, nevertheless, caught some of the glow of religious enthusiasm from the Methodist movement, developed its own school of writers, and set a definite type of evangelical hymnody. Whitefield's hymn

[26] Sankey's "My Life and the Story of the Gospel Hymns" (Sunday School Times Co., Philadelphia, 1906) is of great interest; *cf.* also below, pp. 48-49.

[27] Benson, *op. cit.*, p. 298.

book was published in 1753. It contained twenty
Wesleyan hymns, but more from Dr. Watts. Whitefield's ideal combined Watts' sober dignity and the
fervor and enthusiasm of the Wesleys. This hymnal
was reprinted thirty-six times between 1753 and 1796
and exercised a wide contemporary influence in England. It is important to note that the early evangelical clergy of the Church of England were strongly drawn to this book, which thus became one of the
foundation stones of the earlier group of Episcopal
hymnals. The most important of this group was the
"Olney Hymns", published in 1779 by John Newton,
curate of Olney, and containing two hundred and
eighty of his own hymns, with sixty-eight by his
friend William Cowper. The appeal of this book was
instantaneous and wide, and some of its hymns are
still cherished by Christians everywhere.[28]

Among American Baptists the adoption of the
Whitefield hymnody was delayed, principally because
of the popularity of Dr. Watts, and also by reason
of the addiction of many churches to psalm singing.
But the evangelical hymns were actually introduced

[28] For example, Newton's "How sweet the name of Jesus
sounds"; Glorious things of Thee are spoken"; "Safely through
another week"; "Approach, my soul, the mercy-seat"; "Come,
my soul, thy suit prepare"; "Quiet, Lord, my froward heart";
"While with ceaseless course the sun"; and Cowper's "O for
a closer walk with God"; "God moves in a mysterious way";
"There is a fountain filled with blood"; "Sometimes a light
surprises"; "Jesus, where'er Thy people meet"; "Hark, my
soul, it is the Lord"; "The Spirit breathes upon the Word."

quite generally into Baptist churches before Presbyterians and Congregationalists had come from under
Watts' spell, and while the Episcopalians were still
chanting psalms and the Dutch Reformed bodies singing "Dienet dem Herrn mit Freuden; kommt vor Sein
Angesicht mit Frohlocken." A large number of
hymnals made their appearance, once the evangelical
hymnody was definitely accepted by Baptists. Rippon's "Selection," to which reference has already
been made (pp. 28-29), was reprinted in this country
in 1792. In the West and South, "The Baptist
Hymn Book" (W. C. Buck, Louisville, 1842) was
widely used. In 1843 "The Psalmist" appeared from
a Boston publishing house. One of its compilers was
S. F. Smith, author of "America." This book, containing eleven hundred and eighty hymns, marked a
decided advance in Baptist hymnody. It gave Baptists the precedence over other denominations in
definitely abandoning the period of compromise between psalms and hymns, and, furthermore, it rather
scorned the Baptist predilection for trashy songs.
In the South it was not a success, because of the
omission of a number of popular hymns. In 1850
Dr. Richard Fuller and Dr. J. B. Jeter published
these hymns as a supplement to "The Psalmist." But
in 1851 the Southern Publication Society issued "The
Baptist Psalmody", and this collection, with Sidney
Dyer's "Southwestern Psalmist" (Louisville), prac-

tically closed the field in the South to the Boston publication.

In 1832 a hymn book of a new type appeared, whose editors were Thomas Hastings, a Presbyterian, and Lowell Mason, a Congregationalist. These men attempted to work a reformation in church music by articles and lectures, singing schools, and the training of choirs in the leadership of congregational singing. Their book, "Spiritual Songs for Social Worship", sought to provide words and music adapted to the ability of the average man in the pew, with especial emphasis upon devoutness and spirituality. The book was deservedly popular, and its beneficent influence is still widely felt, for among the original hymns it contained were Hastings' "Hail to the brightness of Zion's glad morning", S. F. Smith's "The morning light is breaking", and Ray Palmer's "My faith looks up to Thee". Mason's tunes (some of them arrangements from musical classics) are universally beloved—and used. The following brief list, in which the names of the respective tunes appear in the parentheses, will show how deeply all denominations are indebted to Lowell Mason for his reverent, devotional, churchly music:[29] "O day of rest and gladness" (Mendebas); "Safely through another week" (Sabbath); "Hark, what

[29] For interesting accounts of tunes as well as poems, consult "The Story of the Hymns and Tunes," Brown and Butterworth (American Tract Society, New York, 1906).

mean these holy voices" (Harwell); "Joy to the world" (Antioch); "When I survey the wondrous Cross" (Hamburg); "Come, let us join our cheerful songs" (Azmon); "There is a fountain" (Cowper); "My faith looks up to Thee" (Olivet); "Nearer, my God, to Thee" (Bethany); "O could I speak the matchless worth" (Ariel); "Father, whate'er of earthly bliss" (Naomi); "Blest be the tie that binds" (Dennis); "My soul, be on thy guard" (Laban); "If through unruffled seas" (Selvin); "Go, labor on" (Ernan); "Work, for the night is coming" (Work Song); "From Greenland's icy mountains" (Missionary Hymn); "God is the refuge of His saints" (Ward).

We have now to consider the Romantic Movement of the early nineteenth century in its relation to hymnology. Among the poets of this remarkable period who wrote hymns and religious poetry were Thomas Moore,[30] Byron, Wordsworth, Coleridge, Scott, and Shelley. Of course these men wrote sacred song only incidentally, and yet their example was not without its immediate effect upon the lesser poets of the day. There was a general effort made to put poetic feeling and literary art more completely at the service of hymn writing. The real leader of this new movement was Bishop Reginald Heber. The

---

[30] Author of "Come, ye disconsolate," one of the most beautiful devotional poems ever written.

claim has, indeed, been made that every hymn he wrote is today in common use. His book, "Hymns written and adapted to the weekly church service of the year", was published posthumously in 1827; and, representing, as it does, the culmination of the literary movement, it offered a new standard of hymnody,—pure devotion accommodated to the church year and expressed with poetic dignity.[31]

One of the most important results of Heber's work was the turning of the tide of hymn singing in the Church of England.[32] Here, at last, were beautiful hymns, composed by a good Tory churchman,—hymns that recognized the holy days of the church year, and that removed from hymnody the undignified "taint" of Methodism and Evangelicalism.

Throughout this period of literary renaissance Baptists clung to their homiletical hymnody,[33] although John Curtis published in 1827 a rather unwieldy Baptist hymnal, containing songs by Coleridge, Scott, Byron, Moore, and Bishop Heber. The modern period of Baptist hymnody may be said to have begun in 1858, when the Particular Baptists

[31] Among Heber's greatest hymns the following may be mentioned: "Holy, Holy, Holy"; "The Son of God goes forth to war"; "Brightest and best of the sons of the morning"; "Bread of the world, in mercy broken"; "From Greenland's icy mountains"; "When thro' the torn sail the wild tempest is streaming"; "Hosanna to the living Lord"; "God that madest earth and heaven."

[32] *Cf.* also p. 50.

[33] See p. 28.

published "Psalms and Hymns prepared for the use of the Baptist Denomination." This book, with a "Supplement", issued some twenty years later, frankly aimed at a high literary standard, and contained hymns by a number of the best writers of the time. In 1866 Mr. Spurgeon issued "Our own hymns", a book which was quite widely used.

Henry Ward Beecher led the way, in this country, to real congregational singing. His "Plymouth Collection of Hymns and Tunes" (1855) did more to take hymn singing out of the hands of the choir and put it where it belongs than any other book ever published. Many Baptist and Presbyterian churches adopted it, though it was issued, of course, under Congregationalist auspices.

Mention must be made here, sadly, of another pioneer of this period, Dr. Charles S. Robinson, who possesses the unenviable distinction of being patron saint to the commercial "hymn" writers of the present day. Dr. Robinson made a business of hymn book compilation, and during the years 1862-1892 he published as many as fifteen books. "Dr. Robinson found his opportunity in the remissness of the church authorities in meeting the needs of the time. Incidentally his labors proved very profitable to him and his publishers and unhappily proved a great stimulus to the commercial side of hymn book making. And a commercialized Hymnody is not a pleasant object of contemplation to any one who cares for the sanctities or the best interests of public worship".[34]

We come now to the "Gospel Hymn", which may be regarded as an offset to the Literary Hymn. The former is the lineal descendant of the old Camp Meeting Hymn and grew at least partly out of the evangelistic work of the Y. M. C. A., organized in Boston in 1851. Tourjée, Phillips, Moody, Doane, Bliss, Sankey, and others, brought the Gospel Hymn into wide popularity during the succeeding years. But Moody's evangelistic campaigns did more, perhaps, to create the tremendous demand for these hymns than any other agency. This demand grew so great that "Gospel Hymns and Sacred Songs", published by Bliss and Sankey in 1875, was followed the next year by "Gospel Hymns, No. 2"; and two years later, by "Gospel Hymns, No. 3". The series ended with "Gospel Hymns, No. 6", issued in 1891. In the opinion of the writer, "Gospel Hymns 1 to 6" is a book of varied merit. There are in it long stretches of the dreariest sort of uninspired dullness, illuminated here and there by a genuine hymn. This statement applies especially to the first part of the book; for the last two or three hundred hymns are, with a few exceptions, deeply and justly loved by many thousands of Christians everywhere.

[34] Benson, *op. cit.,* p. 480.

"It was the lack of any educational idea or development in the 'Gospel Hymns' school of Hymnody that has caused its rapid deterioration. Countless imitators of *Gospel Hymns* were raised up, without the inspiration and sometimes without the unmixed motives of the leaders. Every new evangelist following Moody's methods must have his Sankey and his own hymn book. Moreover, the immense pecuniary success of the *Gospel Hymns* series (in which Moody and Sankey took no share for personal use) offered great temptations to publishers and writers, and the making of such books soon became a trade. They deteriorated partly because the standard of popular music and verse descended to the rag-time level, and partly because it is simpler to deal with the great public on its own plane, or a little below it, than to attempt to uplift it".[35]

We must turn back at this point to consider another great movement which had its beginning in the year which witnessed the culmination of the Literary Movement, and which we may call the Classical, or Oxford, Revival. This revival arose within the Church of England, and John Keble was its founder. His book, "The Christian Year", published in 1827, was rather a collection of meditative verse than a hymnal, and its wide influence was gained by the poetic emphasis placed upon the feasts and fasts of

[35] Benson, *op. cit.*, p. 490.

the church year.[36] There followed a closer study
of the Prayer Book and the Catholic Breviary, and
ere long translations of the Latin hymns contained
in the latter began to appear and to attract deep
interest. The ultimate result was the Liturgical
Hymn. The Church of England had, up to that
time, regarded the hymn with disfavor and scorn,
because it was a mark of Dissent. But now, the
hymn was discovered to be Catholic in origin; and
hymn singing in the Church of England, stimulated
by this discovery, and by the widely recognized worth
of Heber's book, also published in 1827,[37] thence-
forward rested upon an entirely different basis. The
new movement, moreover, revealed to the Church the
great stores of hitherto unknown Latin and Greek
hymns, which were attacked and translated with
vigor and enthusiasm. Finally, it affected the mo-
tive and content of the English Hymn, for it firmly
established the Liturgical Hymn as a distinct type.
The Liturgical Hymn is the voice of the worshiping
church, while the Evangelical Hymn expresses the
aspirations of the individual; the Liturgical Hymn
relates Christian experience to the hour of worship, the church season, the sacrament.

There was, of course, an immediate need of new

[36] Three of Keble's best loved hymns may be mentioned:
"New every morning is the love"; "The voice that breathed
o'er Eden"; "Sun of my soul, Thou Saviour dear."

[37] See p. 46.

hymnals. Space will permit the mention of only two of the men who helped to supply them. After devoting years to a patient study of post-classical Latin, John Mason Neale wrote numerous articles on ecclesiastical Latin poetry and made those remarkable translations of Latin and Greek hymns, so many of which are among our most cherished songs today.[38] Following the publication of Dr. Neale's translations (1851), a number of books were issued, some along the lines laid down by Neale, others representing the Evangelical wing of the Church. In 1859 the Reverend Francis H. Murray secured an agreement with the owners of the more widely used of these hymnals to the effect that they would withdraw their respective books and unite in the preparation of a common collection. This appeared in 1861, under the title, "Hymns ancient and modern for use in the services of the Church". The success of this hymnal is to be compared only with that of Watts' publications and the work of the brothers Wesley. It established the type and tone of Episcopalian hymnody in England, and influenced in no small way the hymnody of Nonconformist bodies.

[38] The following may be mentioned: "The day is past and over"; "Fierce was the wild billow"; "All glory, laud, and honor"; "The day of resurrection"; "Come, ye faithful, raise the strain"; "Christian, dost thou see them"; "Jerusalem the golden"; "Christ is made the sure foundation"; "Safe home, safe home in port"; "O happy band of pilgrims"; "Alleluia, song of gladness"; "O come, O come, Emmanuel"; "For thee, O dear, dear country."

In America, translations of two Latin hymns were published in 1840, and during the subsequent years numerous others appeared and were speedily given place in hymnals of all denominations. Upon Baptists the Oxford influence made only a feeble impression, and the Baptist hymn books of the latter years of the nineteenth century were evangelical and homiletical, rather than liturgical.

In conclusion, we must note some of the characteristics of twentieth century hymnody.

Firstly, although revival influences have profoundly affected hymnody since the beginning, and never more so than during the past ten or fifteen years, very few of the current evangelistic songs have found their way into real hymnals, for two reasons: first, they are of such very poor quality; second, the most popular ones are protected by strict copyrights. Some, indeed, are so precious to their perpetrators that they are guarded by international copyrights!

In the next place, the more exacting literary standards set by the Literary Movement have driven out of circulation many hymns of inferior workmanship. There can be no doubt that in recent years the literary level of hymn books has been notably raised. I refer, of course, to genuine hymn books; not to the collections of dance music and doggerel which desecrate so many of our churches and Sunday schools today—collections whose standards can be improved only by consuming fire.—And in the raising of the literary standard, be it remembered, the devotional level has itself been elevated.

Again, with the passing of the years, the controversial and polemic hymns of the various denominations have, to a very great extent, dropped out of currency, and the general body of hymns sung by all denominations alike has steadily increased.

It must be noted, further, that new ideas of religion and the multiplication of sects and creeds have had their effect upon hymnody. There is a growing use of vernacular hymns in Catholic churches, and hymn singing, with a real hymn book, has been widely introduced into the Quaker meeting. And here is John Hunter, of Glasgow, publishing "Hymns of Faith and Life", and eschewing such dogmatic statements as "God in three Persons, blessed Trinity", and setting the divineness of the present life over against evangelical "otherworldliness". This book, issued in 1889, was the forerunner of much in present day hymnody. Let us take one example, "The Pilgrim Hymnal" (1904), published under Congregationalist auspices. The convictions of a large number of leading men in the denomination were ascertained by a questionnaire, and the book was thus made up with some two hundred men acting as advisers. Here are some of the characteristics of this intensely modern hymnal: First, there is an effort to be strictly "up to date" in terminology. Second, the idea of God's presence *here* is emphasized, as against the older conception of His remoteness, of His enthronement in the heavens. Third, there is an indefiniteness as to the person and nature of Christ. Fourth, the whole tone of the book is distinctly non-ecclesiastical. Fifth, activity, service, are stressed, instead of inward experience. Sixth, hymns that deal with our probationary relation to the future life are avoided. Seventh, and especially characteristic, not only of this particular book, but of the new hymnody in general, social service and humanitarianism loom large.

And so, while our grandfathers and grandmothers sang "When I can read my title clear", the present generation is singing "Where cross the crowded ways of life", and the hymnody of social service, of democracy, of concern for those not in the Church, has come into vigorous being. Indeed, so far, this social, democratic tendency is the twentieth century's contribution to hymnody. Praise and service now go hand in hand.

George Matheson, author of that matchless hymn, "O Love that wilt not let me go", made this statement a few years ago: [39] "To my mind they [our hymns] have one great defect; they lack humani-

---

[39] Quoted by Benson, *op. cit.*, p. 588.

tarianism. There is any amount of doctrine in the Trinity, Baptism, Atonement, or the Christian life as such, but what of the secular life—the infirmary, the hospital, the home of refuge? . . . I don't think our hymns will ever be what they ought to be, until we get them inspired by a sense of the enthusiasm of, and for, humanity. It is rather a theological point, perhaps, but the hymnists speak of the surrender to Christ. They forget that Christ is not simply an individual. He is Head of a body, the body of humanity; and it no longer expresses the idea correctly to join yourself to Christ only; you must give yourself to the whole brotherhood of man to fulfil the idea".

Contemporary hymnody is adapting itself more and more every day to this ideal of worship *and* service; of reverent love for God, *plus* energetic activity for the good of the weak and sinful; of praise and thanksgiving for blessings and for salvation, *together with* earnest striving to bring in now, in the hearts of all men everywhere, the kingdom of our heavenly Father.

CHAPTER II

THERE are, perhaps, a number of reasons, worthy and otherwise, for the singing of hymns in religious services. Variety must be imparted to the program, or the people will be bored; the dozing members of the congregation must be stirred from the borderland of slumber by an impressive noise; the entrance of certain late-comers must be softened and covered by the general participation of the punctual in some sort of exercise; the main point of the sermon must be presented from another angle; the choir must be permitted to display its abilities; the right hand of fellowship must be extended without the embarrassment of silence; new members must be escorted to the front bench by music. But there is only one fundamental reason for the singing of hymns, and that is that the people may worship God.

"God is a Spirit: and they that worship him must worship him in spirit and in truth". Those who believe that statement of Scripture have witnessed with genuine regret and sadness the growing popularity of cheap [1] "hymn" books. During the past ten or fifteen years these books have poured forth from publishing houses and spread over our country in uncounted myriads. In the "Foreword" to one of the most widely used of these publications there are two sentences which may be quoted to convince possible doubters: "The author of this collection has had large experience in compiling song books. His books have gone into churches and Sunday schools by the millions". And he is only one member of a considerable fraternity.

It has already been suggested (in the Preface) that the ignorance and indifference of pastor and people are partly responsible for this most deplorable condition. The consideration of hymns and hymn singing has been neglected shamefully, in view of the fact, which can not be disputed, that the worship of God by the congregation is limited, in most churches, to the singing of the three or four hymns used in the course of the service. Now, worship is too important and vital an exercise to be veiled by the cobwebs of careless disregard and slothfulness. When a new minister is to be called, we consider long and earnestly his past career, his successes and failures, his ability as a preacher, his personal gifts, etc. We pray about the matter and beg the Divine guidance

---

[1] The term, "cheap," refers throughout to quality and not price.

in selecting the right man. All this is as it should be. But when we feel the need of a new hymnal, we submit the worship of God to some slick-tongued agent who usually carries along a load of specious holiness and counterfeit piety as excess baggage, take his word for the wonders of his hymn book, buy the book, forthwith forgot about worshiping God in spirit and in truth, and begin to "worship" Him in ragtime and in jig. Our ancestors were so considerate of the proprieties of the sanctuary that for centuries they used only the actual words of Scripture in their songs. We, now, will use anything, be it never so cheap and unholy.

There are some other reasons for the rapid advance of cheap "hymns" into popular favor, which it will be well to note.

In the first place, they are extensively and very shrewdly advertised. And this advertising is not done through newspapers in any large degree. At nearly every denominational gathering (I speak particularly of Baptists here) cheap books are used,— are "furnished" by the publisher. How generous! For example, a certain book was "furnished" for a recent meeting of North Carolina Baptist State Convention. A few days after the Convention had closed, a communication appeared in the Baptist State paper from the pastor of the church in which the Convention had met, to the effect that he had forgotten to announce that the books furnished by Bro. So-and-So were for sale at such and such a price! Two or three years ago I was invited to conduct the music at an important denominational gathering in another State. Some weeks before the time set for the meeting I received a letter, written with evident embarrassment, opining that, inasmuch as Bro. Blank had kindly agreed to furnish hymn books, I would probably like to be excused!

Now the simple truth of the matter is that all this generous "furnishing" is done for the sole purpose of advertising the book; and no man can dispute the effectiveness of the method. Of course, no publisher with the slightest regard for the proprieties and sanctities of worship would think for a moment of advertising in such a manner; but the cheap "hymn" book publishers, not being famous for the possession of this quality, are but running true to type in piously "furnishing" with a view to remuneratively selling.

Not only are cheap books advertised at denominational gatherings, but nearly every evangelistic singer, so far as my observation goes, uses them, and many sell them.[2] Dear reader, have you ever listened to a quack doctor expatiating upon the excellencies of his nostrum? If so, you have invariably heard him conclude something like this: "Now,

---

[2] *Cf.* Dr. Benson's remarks, quoted above, p. 49.

friends, you can find out all about what ails you, and how to cure it, in my little book here; price only fifty cents." Were you ever among those present at an exhibition of mind-reading? If so, you were exposed to some such peroration as this: "Now, friends, you can find out all about my wonderful powers, and how you may develop similar gifts, by a perusal of my little book here; price, only fifty cents." Neither the quack doctor nor the mind-reader could be induced upon any consideration to invade the house of God with *their* books; but the professional singer hails the opportunity, and he is quite willing to degrade and prostitute the sanctuary and defile the worship of God by howling *his* wares from the very Holy of Holies. Jesus, once upon a time, with a scourge, drove from the temple the money-changers, and those that bought and sold in His Father's House.

In some sections of the South "singing conventions" are quite popular. The people come together from all parts of the surrounding country, bring the babies and abundant baskets of dinner, and spend the day (or, sometimes, several days) whooping and squalling and bellowing songs out of sundry cheap books. Various "singing teachers" are on hand, each extolling the glittering merits of the book for which he is agent, and vieing with his fellows in oily piety and in those acrobatic and vulgar antics that are deemed necessary to the successful leadership of choir and congregational singing.

Individual "hymns" receive valuable advertising by their adoption as "official" songs. For example, the B. Y. P. U. of one of the Southern States expresses its ideals through the medium of a cheap little ditty, called "As a Volunteer".—When the Seventy-five Million Campaign was set on foot by Southern Baptists, a certain gentleman wrote a "Campaign Hymn" which was shipped all over the South by the bale. It was called "When Millions come pouring in", and it was of a cheapness and sorriness indescribable. To make bad matters worse, the ingenious gentleman had seized upon the music of the noble "Battle Hymn of the Republic" as a vehicle for his "poem". Some months ago one of our humorous weeklies published "a page of Old Masters as the Sunday Supplement artists of the present time would have painted them". Among these interesting pictures was "The Angelus", with Mutt and Jeff as the two figures in the foreground,—the latter in the act of plunging a pitchfork into the unsuspecting anatomy of his friend. The "Campaign Hymn", with its superb borrowed music and its jangling words, belongs in the same category precisely.

Perhaps the chief reason, however, for the popularity of the cheap "hymn" is to be found in the fondness for secular music of the same type, which seems to be so characteristic of our time. Jazz, waltzes, "Blues", ragtime, slushy sentimentality, have become the musical expression of so many of our people *outside* the church, that the same sort of thing, with a poor, thin veneer of religion, is demanded *in* the church.[3] Cheap secular songs have secured such a strangle hold upon the feelings and affections of church members that they can not stand to be deprived of their favorite musical and sentimental (not to say intellectual) nutriment even in the place of prayer and praise. And just as the silk-shirted young gentlemen of Tin Pan Alley must work far beyond ethical Union hours to supply the demand for secular twaddle such as "Though she's only a moonshiner's daughter, say, boys, I love her still", "I never knew what a wonderful wife I had till the town went dry", and "If I knock the L out of Kelly, why he'll knock the 'ell out of me", so the prosperous members of the Religious Ragtime Association are always happily grinding out new "hymns", such as "There's a question we must settle (vote it out!)" [Tune, "Here's to good old Yale, drink it down"], "Sinsick souls are dying fast", and "O get ye on to Canaan", to supply the equally voracious demand for "sacred" twaddle. New books simply *must* be published every little while to meet this demand; for,

[3] *Cf.* pp. 30-31 and 41, above.

somehow, cheap songs, secular and sacred, wear out rather quickly, like cheap clothes, and others must always be on tap in a sufficient quantity (quality appears to be of no importance) to guarantee the perpetuity of prosperity for the perpetrators and happiness for the users.

If some courageous person were to urge these publishers of sacred rags to start a campaign for the elevation of public taste in the matter of songs for the worship of God, he would be lucky to escape with a whole skin. Elevate public taste, indeed! It is vastly easier and more profitable to pander to it; for if it were elevated, there would soon be no market for cheap "hymn" books.

A quotation from another "Foreword" will show clearly the feelings of these publishers and compilers as to the sublime merits of their wares, and will also exhibit in all its ugliness the mercenary attitude that characterizes the whole fraternity: "A lengthy foreword is unnecessary, as the friends will or should examine a book carefully before selecting. This is all that we ask for this book, and *we earnestly seek comparison with any book in all songland.* Many months have been devoted to careful selection from multiplied thousands of songs; faithful counsel has been sought and obtained from faithful Pastors and experienced Evangelists and Song Leaders; *and much money has been expended in securing the copy-*

rights desired—in fact not a single song selected has been omitted because *the price was too high, although large sums were asked for some of these very popular favorites.*

"We do not ask friends to select this book simply because it has more pages or a larger number of selections than any other book that *sells for the same price,* but we do believe that we have here the *best compilation of Gospel Hymns and Sunday School Songs that has ever been compiled.*

"A number of these songs are herein published for the first time; examine these and the others not so familiar to you, and you will find that there is not a 'filler' in the book".[4]

There you have the whole sorry business, thoughtful reader, set forth in unmistakable terms. And the pious paragraph with which the above "foreword" closes (which I have omitted in order not to identify the book) is wholly out of place in a discussion of "large sums" and "the same price".

I know, of course, that I shall be severely criticised for calling in question the disinterested piety and religious enthusiasm of these gentry. That is neither here nor there, however, for the facts are on my side. Let us consider them.

Worship embraces preaching, prayer and song, and no man can say which is most important. Ser-

---

[4] The italics in this quotation are mine.

mons and prayers are not turned out wholesale by publishing houses, copyrighted, and hawked up and down the land by howling, prancing evangelistic singers. Why should hymns be thus handled? When a volume of sermons is published, the author, or compiler, does not inform a listening and awestruck world that he has the best volume of sermons ever issued, nor does he have any occasion to refer to the "large sums" asked for "popular favorites". A preacher who should write sermons for money would be justly despised by everybody. We have, in our great hymnals, songs which express devoutly and beautifully every feeling of worship that can possibly arise in the breasts of Christians,—songs that grew out of genuine spiritual experience,[5] and not out of the desire for a more impressive bank account. And yet, cheap "hymn" writers continue to turn out songs. Now, if the author of a poem or a tune were really desirous of seeing his production blessed in the bringing in of the Kingdom, he would not be so anxious to get under the wing of the great god copyright, nor would he ask "large sums" for the use of his precious ditty in a forthcoming book. And if publishers were as interested in evangelizing the world through hymns as they claim to be, they would not be so eager to buy the copyrights of popular

[5] For stories of the great hymns, consult Dr. S. W. Duffield's "English Hymns: their Authors and History," Funk and Wagnalls, New York, 1886.

songs and to boost their bank accounts by issuing new collections every year or two.

The demand for cheap "hymns" began to be felt, as has already been suggested, when cheap secular music became popular, and these song writers and publishers are doing their best (or, rather, their worst) to supply the demand. The miserable stuff they turn out will last only a relatively short time, being cheap,[6] and the Church or Sunday school will be looking for a new book. It is always ready. A short time ago an advertisement appeared in one of our religious papers, urging readers to send for "a copy of our new hymn book for 1920, '——, No. 5' ". In other words, the making of these "hymns" and the publishing of these books has become a vastly remunerative trade,[7] and those who profit by it are pushing it to the limit. Now, I, for one, have no objection to the accumulation of wealth by any man, so long as he is honest, *and* so long as he keeps his hands off of the service of the sanctuary. These cheap songs are bad enough *per se*, in all conscience; and when to their inherent sorriness is added the fact that men, through them, are making money out of the degradation of the worship of God, they become unbearable.

The small minority of the tawdry fraternity who

[6] *Cf.* p. 63.
[7] *Cf.* Benson, quoted above, p. 49.

are not writing for money, but who really think they are producing genuine hymns, deserve no censure; rather they are in sore need of pity and enlightenment.

The method of construction of a cheap "hymn" is precisely the same as that employed in the composition of the secular song of the same type. The "poet" gets an idea around which to write his words. This idea is almost invariably expressed in the chorus, to which the verses bear more or less relation.[8] For instance, a gifted and popular moving picture actor recently returned to the United States from Honolulu. In a conversation with one of his friends with regard to feminine costume among the islanders, he remarked, "They are wearing them higher in Hawaii". Forthwith one of the inmates of Tin Pan Alley (referred to above) turned out a song upon that edifying theme, the chorus of which insisted again and again, almost to the point of weariness and indecency, that they were wearing them higher in Hawaii. The rest of the song did not matter. "Love lifted me", "Brighten the corner", and "There is power in the Blood" are fine examples of "sacred" songs composed after the same fashion. The chorus is the main feature. Indeed, it is the main feature of nearly all cheap songs, for church

[8] *Cf.*, for example, that egregious piece of slush, "Just keep sweet," the verses of which, after the first, have nothing whatever in common with the refrain.

or home or dance hall consumption (*cf.* p. 72, below). Any observant person will notice at once, when he hears a song of this type perpetrated in the house of God, that the congregation mumbles the verses and bellows the chorus.

There is a "negro spiritual" that always occurs to me in this connection. It is called "Little David", and its words are as follows:

1. Little David was a shepherd boy,
   He killed Goliath an'-a shout for joy.
   Cho. Little David, play on your harp,
       Hallelu', Hallelu',
   Little David, play on your harp,
       Hallelu!

2. Joshua was the son of a Nun,
   He never would stop till the work was done.
       Chorus.

3. O, I tell you once, I tell you twice,
   There are sinners in hell for shootin' dice.
       Chorus.

Now, it will be observed that this classic deserts its text, as it were. Surely; but that makes little difference. Numbers of our cheap "hymns" show a like desertion,—differing only in degree. Really, you are supposed to say "Tum-te-tum-te-tum", etc., until you arrive at the chorus, when you are expected to get under a full head of steam immediately, and roar, "Bright-ún the cor-núr *whére yóu áre*", etc., etc. It may be remarked, incidentally, that that very popular song offers a sorry ideal to our ambitious young people today.

The music of the cheap "hymn" now demands our attention, and it may be said at the outset that the "composers" are far more responsible for the sorriness of the combined product than the "poet". The words of the song may be but poor doggerel and sentimentality; the verses may show only a distant kinship to the chorus; the grammar may be (and often is) nauseating; but there is always enough religion about them to give the thoughtful singer at least a vague impression that he is rendering something which was intended to be a sacred song. But the "composers" have abandoned utterly the spirit of worship, and have fled, bag and baggage, to the dance hall,[9] the musical comedy, and the cheap movie for their inspiration. The result is that thousands of our churches and Sunday schools are using the *same sort of music exactly* as is jingled forth by the electric piano at the picture house, the pony ballet in the theatre, and the jazz orchestra in the public dance hall. Of course the music makes the popularity of all songs, good and bad, and it has been suggested already that our people like "sacred" music

[9] At a dance held two or three years ago in an Eastern North Carolina city, the orchestra used "hymns" from one cheap book the whole evening.

of the ragtime type because of their fondness for similar secular stuff.

We set great store, in our moral teaching, by association. The card table is wrong because of its immemorial connection with gambling; the pool table is to be shunned because it long occupied the back room of the saloon. Now, how can a devout Christian worship God by singing a waltz? How can a sorry piece of ragtime carry a prayer upward to the Throne? How, in heaven's name, can a one-step, beslimed with the sensual postures of a dance hall, make its way, as the bearer of holy adoration, above the earth and into the pure air of the New Jerusalem? There is a place for waltzes, ragtime and one-steps, but it is not the church of the living God.

Let me illustrate. One of the most popular songs (for which "large sums" are asked) in the repertoire of the itinerant singer is called "Saved! Saved!" It is a waltz, thinly disguised by twelve-eight time, and a fairly good waltz, too. I have not discovered the source of the music employed for the verses, but the chorus is an adaptation of the same portion of that once popular ballad, "I wisht I wuz single again",—an adaptation, it may be said,—which departs very slightly from the original fount of inspiration. Play it over, and be convinced, if you doubt. The author of this song liked its music so well that about five years later he repeated it in another waltz, called "Wonderful Name". A more proper title would be "Wonderful Similarity". No. 2 is written in a different key, but laying that alteration aside, it is No. 1, almost note for note, even down to a sliding stunt for the alto in the chorus.

The term, ragtime, is technically used to refer to rapid and frequent syncopation. Ragtime music was first popularized by Kerry Mills, composer of "Whistlin' Rufus", "Georgia Camp Meetin' ", "Happy Days in Dixie", etc. Innumerable writers have flooded the country with ragtime, good and bad, since Mills' day (some twenty years ago), and the concocters of cheap "hymns" have not by any means been left behind the band wagon. Three or four measures of "Brighten the corner" will illustrate the use of syncopation in "hymns":

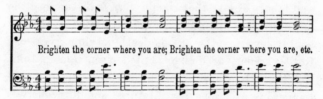

Brighten the corner where you are; Brighten the corner where you are, etc.

The syllables *-en* of *brighten* and *-ner* of *corner* are syncopated twice each in those four measures.[10]

Worse, however, than the waltz or the ragtime,

[10] For the sake of clearness I have written the second measure simply, omitting a hair-raising nose dive and spiral ascent for the bass, which occurs in the printed song.

is the jingle, for it scrapes the mud off the very bottom of the slough of cheapness. And, strange to say, the jingle is far more popular for "sacred" than for secular songs. Here is a sample (words omitted) :

This is a movement exceedingly precious to the souls of our dear "hymn" composers.

One more general characteristic of these songs must be noted. Not only do almost all of them possess a chorus, as the main feature (*cf.* p. 67, above), but that chorus is subjected to those adornments and labors of love that should always distinguish the most precious things in life. It contains gymnastic contortions for the basso, death-defying gyrations for the tenor, or double-jointed circumambulations for the alto—sometimes, to be sure, frantic and dangerous exertions for all three simultaneously— while the soprano bravely pegs away at the tune. Truly, it is marvelous and inspiring to hear!

These three types, then, the waltz, the ragtime, the jingle, with the usual acrobatic chorus, will be found to make up nine-tenths of the cheap "sacred"

songs that pour forth every year in a muddy flood
that threatens to engulf all genuine worship.

We may now consider the publisher's side of the
question. He is issuing books as a trade, just as the
majority of song writers are grinding out individual
songs. He is concerned with the prosperity of his
business, he makes it a point to keep in touch with
the market, and he estimates carefully and usually
correctly how long a new product will last. He may
not have admitted, even to himself, that the quality
of the stuff he turns out determines its longevity;
but he knows that, somehow, it does not last long,
and he rejoices thereat, since he can sell more
books. Let us suppose that "Sounding Brass No.
1" was issued early this year. Before the ink is dry
the publisher is making his plans for "Sounding
Brass No. 2", to be put on the market as soon as
the sales of S. B. No. 1 begin to show a marked decline. His preparation includes the purchase of as
many popular songs as he can buy, the expenditure
of "large sums" for the use of those he can not get
outright, careful investigation of the relative popularity of the songs in S. B. No. 1, "faithful counsel
from faithful Pastors and experienced Evangelists
and Song Leaders",—*and* counting of the profits.
When the time is ripe, that is, when churches and
Sunday schools seem about ready to make a change
in books, S. B. No. 2 is sent forth with great pomp

and circumstance. Let us glance at its contents.
It opens with a preface, or "foreword", written either
by the compiler, or, if his vocabulary was exhausted
in extolling the merits of S. B. No. 1, by some very
influential minister. Then follow the songs. The
more popular ones from S. B. No. 1 are reprinted,
with enough new productions to justify the change
in the title, and to impart an aspect of novelty to
the book. Over in the back, in miserable, small type,
and ignominiously treated as a sort of caudal ap-
pendage, are fifty or more real hymns to serve as a
sop to the feelings of that minority who still believe
in spiritual worship in song.

These good hymns do not cost the publisher "large
sums", for they were written for the glory of God.
In many of these books the section (at the rear)
containing the real songs of worship is headed "Devotional Hymns". Lo! the poor compilers, hoist on
their own petard! *All hymns ought to be devotional.*

I have before me a cheap hymnal, published two
years ago, in which the genuine hymns are better
treated as to type and are scattered through the
book. That is a great improvement, as I am glad to
admit, though to be sure I should think the good
hymns would prefer to flock by themselves, bad type
or no, rather than to be surrounded by such sorry
company.

The process outlined above is repeated at more or less regular intervals, the market is always flooded with a steady stream of Sounding Brasses, the profits pile up, and everybody is happy, except those who grieve at the spectacle of the worship of God brought down to the level of the street and the dance hall by the depravity of popular taste and the willingness of writers and publishers to pander to it for the sake of unholy gain. "Thou shalt not take the name of the Lord thy God in vain" may surely be paraphrased to read, "Thou shalt not use unworthily the name of the Lord thy God, for the sake of increasing thy store of the mammon of unrighteousness".

A session with these books under the leadership of a singer who loves them (for one reason or another) is a sight for the gods. The whole performance would not last one night at any cheap vaudeville show in the land. The singer marches up on the platform, cracks a few venerable jokes, unlimbers his muscles and his larynx and announces a "hymn". Then, while the audience turn over the pages in the search for the gem with which they are about to approach the throne of God, the singer gets a few more hand-picked classics out of his system. Everybody being at last ready, the pianist reels off a few measures (keeping time with as much of his anatomy as he can move without precipitating himself from his seat), the people get their feet into action, and the worship of God begins.

It continues until time for the Scripture, or until the jokes give out, or until the singer grows weary of waving his arms around in the frantic effort to keep the songs up to good dance hall tempo. Pleasantries are exchanged between singer and audience, such as, "All the good-looking young ladies under thirty are requested to sing the next verse, the men joining in the chorus", etc., etc., etc. On a certain Sunday last year the writer attended the Sabbath school in one of the greatest churches in the South. The superintendent, dissatisfied with the manner in which the audience sang the first "hymn", proposed that they should whistle it, which they did with alacrity. It is needless to say that the song was a cheap jig. No one out of a lunatic asylum would ever think of suggesting that "Jesus, lover of my soul" should be whistled in a religious service.

Such performances are disgraceful and sacrilegious beyond the power of words to express, and yet they are going on all over the land, every Sunday in the year.

We may now examine the arguments usually advanced for the use of cheap "hymns".

Firstly, "the books cost less money than real hymnals". How often have we all heard that piece of shallow sophistry! To be sure they cost less money at the outset. But by the time the church or Sunday school has bought new books two or three times in the space of four or five years, it has spent much more than would have been required for a good hymn book that would last indefinitely.

Secondly, "the people tire of the 'old' hymns". Yes, they frequently do. And when that happens, you may be sure that one or more of three reasons is responsible. Either a very few hymns have been sung over and over, or they have been senselessly dragged to death by a lazy choir and a still lazier congregation, or some enemy of the true worship of God has been sowing tears. The remedy is, of course, the learning of more good hymns, a little more energy and spirit in choir and congregation, and a cold shoulder to the enemy.

Thirdly, "these songs are not so difficult to sing as the standard hymns". That statement, made so often in defense of trash, is wholly false, as can be proven by anybody who knows enough music to sit down at the piano and play over songs of both types. "Onward, Christian soldiers" is very much easier to play and sing than "The fight is on". The lovely harmony of "O Jesus, Thou art standing" is infinitely simpler than the cumbersome waltz measures of "Let Jesus come into your heart". Examples might be multiplied indefinitely. The cheap song,

with its jingling, jigging verses and its rantankerous
chorus, requires considerably more musical (not to
say acrobatic) ability for its rendition than does
a devotional, worshipful hymn; and the proponents
of the ditty need never attempt to substantiate the
contrary to any pastor who is at all musical, and
still less to a director of music who can distinguish
between A flat and B flat.

We are told, too, that the sentiments expressed
in the standard hymns, "used and defended by high-
falutin folks", are over the heads of the great masses
of the people, who must, therefore, have songs of
a lower literary grade. I do not believe that
wretched slander, and I challenge any jigster on
earth to prove it. There is not a man or woman,
boy or girl, in any of our churches unable to com-
prehend the meaning of "My faith looks up to Thee",
or "Joy to the world", or "The Homeland", or
"Stand up, stand up for Jesus", or "Day is dying
in the West", or "The King of Love my Shepherd
is". "The defenders of this popular hymnody . . .
often very gravely underestimate the capacity of
the popular mind to rise above vulgar embodiments
of truth and to shake itself free from perverted sentimentality".[11]   I should like to alter Professor
Pratt's statement slightly, so as to have it read, "The

[11] Pratt, *op. cit.*, p. 60.

defenders of this popular hymnody . . . often succeed in causing pastors and musical directors very gravely to underestimate", etc. Devout Christians may well be insulted at such a thinly disguised insinuation of feeble-mindedness as is conveyed by the glib patter of some book agent who contends that they can not apprehend the true inwardness of "In the cross of Christ I glory" and "All hail the power of Jesus' name".

A fourth argument employed with particular frequency and zest by advocates of cheap "hymns" is that they stir up "the pep". They do. But the "pep" thus engendered is a poor, specious counterfeit of that deep religious enthusiasm aroused by the hearty singing of a real hymn. It may well be doubted very seriously whether "pep" is a needful commodity for religious bodies, anyway. Enthusiasm, zeal, energy, are invaluable, and the more we have of them, the sooner will the Kingdom of God become an accomplished fact. But "pep" somehow suggests the cheering section at a college baseball game, or a hustling salesman, or a ranting chautauqua lecturer. Laying aside, however, the more or less slender difference of meaning between the words "pep" and "enthusiasm", I maintain that the results in religious fervor claimed for cheap songs may not only be equalled, but surpassed, through the use

of good songs.[12] Not long ago I received from a
Presbyterian pastor a letter, one paragraph of
which is pertinent at this point: "I am more im-
pressed with the necessity for it [the study of hym-
nology] than ever, because I have just closed a meeting for a brother pastor, a young man, who is a good
singer and a good song leader, but I had to tell him
perfectly plainly that some of the stuff he was teaching those people to sing for music and for worship
disgusted me, made a farce of the whole thing, and
absolutely sent me to my sermon with every vestige
of real worship gone from me. We then took up
the old hymns and the entire spirit of the meeting
changed. After he had made them sing 'Brighten
the corner', etc., I raised 'There is a fountain filled
with blood,' and everybody got out of the corner,
got together, began to worship, and God came down
to us".

Pardon another personal experience. On a Sunday morning last summer I attended a large Baraca
class in a Southern city. The pianist told me she
did not sympathize with my attitude toward popular
hymnody, and that she liked for the men in the class
to sing "stirring songs". About fifteen minutes later
we had a "stirring song" announced,—that cheap,

---

[12] Pratt, *op. cit.*, p. 60, says: "They [the defenders of cheap
songs] constantly mistake the zest of animal enjoyment in a
rub-a-dub rhythm or the shout of childish pleasure in a 'catchy'
refrain for real religious enthusiasm."

tawdry march already mentioned, "The fight is on". Since there were no professional acrobats in the class, the men simply looked at the verses, while the lady worked diligently at the piano. When they reached the chorus, a few raised their voices feebly, and the only part of the "stirring hymn" that seemed to give general satisfaction was the end. Now, if "The Son of God goes forth to war" had been the selection, the state of mind of the men in that class would have been quite different at the conclusion of the hymn.

The simple truth of the matter is, of course, that singers and publishers have diligently spread abroad the miserably false idea that there is no enthusiasm, or "pep", in the great hymns; that congregations can not be aroused to spiritual activity by the "old songs"; in short, that the only remedy which can cure a church of religious lethargy is jazz, waltz, and "sacred" ragtime. So assiduously has this wretched and poisonous heresy been disseminated that thousands of people actually believe it.

Reference has already been made to the almost universal use of cheap song books by evangelistic singers. A protracted meeting nowadays is frequently a queer affair, being a sort of mixture of religion and buffoonery, the devout spirit of worship and the spicy aroma of the dance hall, the sober presentation of the Word of God and the vulgar antics of the vaudeville clown. Again I beg to submit that just as many souls would be saved, and saved far more genuinely, *and far more decently*, if "Just as I am, without one plea" were sung, instead of "What a gath'ring that will be", with its tinkling verses and three-ring circus chorus.

Permit me to repeat that, in the protracted meeting, or in the regular services of the church or Sunday school, more enthusiasm and enthusiasm of an infinitely higher character can be aroused by the vigorous singing of a good hymn than by the equally vigorous rendition of a poor one. And if tenderness, devoutness, contrition, prayerfulness, are to be sought through the service of song, nobody in his right mind would or could propose a piece of sorry ragtime as the agent of their stimulation.

A recent issue of *The Congregationalist* contains the following brief and forceful article, under the heading, "Better music for the youth of today":

"Prof. Augustine Smith in his leadership of the music at the International Council gave a practical demonstration of how completely the standard hymns of the church lend themselves to worship. He showed that it is not at all necessary to use religious ragtime to the accompaniment of a trick pianist with the leading of a clown to make music worshipful. He not only brought out the message of the musical setting of the hymns, but he also interpreted wonderfully the poets who wrote them. For two or three years he has been rendering this same sort of service to the country through the conventions of the International Sunday School Association. In other years the association was not so fortunate in its leadership because the musical leaders tried to make the music a performance rather than an act of worship. In many of the conventions held by the association also no attempt apparently was made to teach the delegates how to make the music in the home church the most worshipful.

"In a large convention held by another interdenominational organization we could not help contrasting the music with that led by Prof. Smith at Boston. The book used was put out by the publishing house of the organization and its preface was written by one of the foremost Christian leaders. The hymns in the book are not representative of the best music of the church, and the singing was led by a man who acted more the part of a clown than that of a leader of music in a Christian gathering. The pianist was a trick player, whose 'dives' and 'uppercuts' tended to destroy what worshipful spirit there might have been in the large number of youth present. The convention was for young people. It is a crime when the music of a Christian gathering is treated as an opportunity for personal or technical display and not as a means and an ideal of worship for youth.

"Prof. Smith has proved conclusively that young people will sing heartily the best hymns of the church if they have the proper leadership. It is time for the great interdenominational organizations to demand that their youth in the impressionable period be given the best music under the most reverent leadership, not only in order that they may learn how to worship, but that they may fill their memory with hymns worth retaining. We ought to have a change in the kind of music provided for our youth and we ought to have it at once."

Many thoughtful Christians have deeply deplored the rapid growth of irreverence for sacred things and sacred places, particularly among the younger generation. There is no doubt in my own mind that this most unfortunate condition is due very largely to the irreverent way in which we worship God in song in so many of our meetings. How, in all seriousness, can a boy be expected to maintain a reverent attitude toward the Sunday morning service, when the "hymns" that are sung are so insistently reminiscent of the dance he attended the night before, or of the piano at the picture show which he patronized the preceding week? If the songs, his only medium of participation in the service, are jazzy, how can his feeling toward the service be reverent?

Yet another argument frequently submitted for cheap "hymns" is that the people like them. That is quite true, unfortunately. Many people like whisky, also. But whisky has been outlawed, not only by Constitutional amendment but also by public opinion, and people who like it are either developing a taste for other beverages or intrusting their lives to the doubtful contents of the blockader's jug. Is this an unfair illustration? Not at all. Whisky was outlawed because it was found to exert a deleterious effect upon the human body. The human soul is a far more important thing than the fleshly envelope in which it resides. And if the cheap song degrades the worship of God, then it also degrades that spiritual essence within us *through which alone* we *can* worship. Surely we have trifled and piddled long enough, with this cancer eating at the heart of the service of praise and thanksgiving. The time has come to pluck it out and cast it from us and to consider deeply and carefully how we may better worship God in spirit and in truth.

Again, we have all heard remarks like this: "Yes, there is a lot of trash in that 'Sanctified Jazz No. 19', but it contains a lot of standard hymns, too". That sort of statement is hardly to be dignified by the word "argument"; it is a kind of excuse for the cheap book, and a very poor excuse, too. Why compromise? The only thing to do is to use a book that contains good hymns exclusively, and there are many of them. Use the two types of songs side by side; the popular taste for trash will in the majority of cases shuffle the real hymns permanently into the background. Remove the trash absolutely and use only genuinely worshipful songs; soon you will have so far elevated the appreciation of the people as to make even erstwhile devotees of trash rejoice in the deeply spiritual worship of God. The one sure means of accomplishing this result is, as suggested above, the steady use of a book that offers no cheap songs whatsoever.

Another variety of compromise is found in many churches and pushed for all it is worth by the publishers of cheap books. A good hymnal is used for both the church services (though there are many churches in which, for some unknown and abstruse reason, trash is dragged out for the evening worship), but for the Sunday school some sorry job lot of dance music is favored. Now, such a compromise as that is especially poisonous, for the simple reason that our young folks have their taste for sacred song formed almost entirely in the Sunday school, and if they are trained there to love trash, trash they must have when they come into the church. And so, of course, the cheap publishers encourage this compromise, like the keen business men they are, for "train up a child in the way he should go, and when he is old he will not depart from it" is just as true if another "not" be inserted before "go".

There has been some little discussion recently as to the tendency of young people to attend Sunday school and various and sundry religious societies and "circles", and to absent themselves from the church service. It has been suggested by high and expert authorities that the remedy for this unfortunate condition is the alteration of the church service to suit the demands of the young people. This can mean one thing, and one thing only, and that is the lowering of the devotional standards of the Lord's house, through the introduction of cheap hymns (where they are not already in use) and various other unworthy devices to charm a variegated array of half-baked tastes. I do not believe that even this miserable compromise will solve the problem, for it is just as vital in churches that have thus surrendered the true spirit of worship as in those that have not. The only solution, in my opinion, lies in a proper attention to the correct training of the boys and girls *in the Sunday school*. If there are decorum and dignity and the genuine spirit of worship there (and this is not in the least incompatible with youthful enthusiasm), then the transition to the church service is natural and easy. On the other hand, if reverence is undermined and all but destroyed by cheap songs and sundry little stunts and antics, then the church service will appear stiff and solemn and not to be endured. In other words, what we need is not the alteration of the church service to suit the fancy of the young people, but the training of the young people into a reverence and love for the church service. And the Sunday school is the proper and the natural place for this training.

So far as hymns are concerned, there is no earthly reason why one book should be used in church and a different (and sorry) one in the Sunday school. The children *can be trained* to love the good hymns;[13] and we are exceedingly remiss in our duty to them when we expend all our energies in superintending their mental development during the week, only to expose them on Sunday morning to reverence-killing and soul-dwarfing trash in the shape of unworshipful songs. The whole problem of the cheap "hymn" would be solved, and the publishers and writers thereof driven to the wall, or to reformation, if Sunday schools everywhere would sing only genuine hymns.

This chapter began with the statement that the hymn is, above all other considerations, an act of worship. Let us return to that point briefly.

[13] There are innumerable truly worshipful songs whose beauty and whose message can be grasped by children far more completely than some of their elders, who delight to stuff the childish mind and heart with trash, conceive. *Cf.* also the article quoted above, pp. 82-84.

It should be our ideal and purpose to approach God's throne with our prayer and praise as reverently and worshipfully as in us lies. We have no right to use an unworthy vehicle for our devotions,[14] even if some of us do prefer it. Our Lord is no mumbo-jumbo deity to be propitiated with dance hall ditties; He merits and demands the best and the noblest offerings of worship that we can bring, and the emotions and aspirations that ascend to Him on the pinions of song are too divine, too sacred, to be degraded and defiled by the cheap jingle of the street. A minstrel show in the choir loft and a buck-and-wing stunt in the pulpit would not be one whit more sacrilegious than some of the hymns that are sung in choir lofts and some of the contortions perpetrated in pulpits all over this land. For the minstrel and the buck-and-wing are frankly secular, while cheap songs are doggerel and sentimentality and jig masquerading for money in sacred robes; and the ancient jokes and wild gyrations of song leaders are poor vaudeville acts parading under the guise of religious enthusiasm. Harsh words, surely. Yes; we have coddled and pampered these noxious weeds in the garden of the Lord long enough, and the time has come for sound thinking and straight talking. There is no ragtime plank in the divine platform of

---

[14] Read, in this connection, the first chapter of the prophecy of Malachi.

salvation; the mouldy, rotten log of worship on
which so many Christians are standing was rolled
up to the platform by man for man's glory, and it
has tainted the spiritual atmosphere with its rank
fungi of worldliness and crawling vermin of dollar-
chasing far too long. Let us break it to pieces and
destroy it in the fire of genuine religious fervor,
while we sing worthily unto God the great songs of
Zion!

How, it may be asked, are genuine hymns to be
distinguished [15] from cheap imitations? By apply-
ing one or more of three tests.

First, the test of time. I do not mean to imply,
of course, that all old hymns are good, while all new
ones are bad. But if only the songs that have survived all the pruning and winnowing of hundreds of
learned and devout men, and that are found in every
real hymnal of all denominations, are sung, the worship of God is perfectly safe. We use frequently
the phrase, "the good old hymns", and we signify
thereby songs of the type of "Am I a soldier of the
cross"; "O God, our help in ages past"; "Majestic
sweetness sits enthroned"; "Blest be the tie that
binds"; "Rock of Ages"; and the like. *Those* are
the hymns that have survived all the tests that can

[15] There are, of course, some songs about which persons of
the best taste would differ. These, however, form a comparatively small group.

be applied, and that are still fragrant with the Divine Presence.

Secondly, there is a real and vital spiritual instinct that will always function with unerring accuracy, unless it has been put to sleep with the drugs of mercenary hymnody. Refer a hymn to that instinct; ask its judgment upon the worshipfulness of the hymn,—words and music. Suppose you desire to sing about heaven. Set before your spiritual instinct, "I will shout His praise in glory (so will I, so will I)", and let its jingling measures resound in your ears. If you recover from the shock, find "Jerusalem, the golden"; read the wonderful, devotional words and listen to the dignified, beautiful music of the tune "Ewing". Then decide which of the two songs best expresses your idea of heaven.

Suppose, again, you want to praise God for His grace that brought you salvation. Here is "Only a sinner, saved by grace". It begins "Naught have I gotten but what I received" (a marvelous clause whose meaning no man can tell), rambles on through four ungrammatical and illogical verses (and a ragtime chorus), and closes with this gem of linguistic distortion: "Once more to tell it, would I embrace!" Or examine " 'Whosoever' meaneth me"; and weep. I can not refrain from quoting the chorus of this unutterably cheap ditty. It will illustrate quite clearly the poetic genius of the author: " 'Whoso-ever', surely meaneth me, surely meaneth me, O surely meaneth me; 'Whosoever', surely meaneth me, 'whosoever', meaneth me (meaneth me)". Now, compare with those two precious jigs the majestic strains of "All hail the power of Jesus' name", or the inspiring worshipfulness of "Crown Him with many crowns". Your instinct can not lead you astray. Examples might be multiplied indefinitely.

Thirdly, the surest and best test [16] by which to determine the quality of a hymn is, of course, the test of mature judgment. If your judgment is immature or biased, dear reader, don't admit it by supercilious ridicule of those who, with the interest of the worship of God at heart, are trying to rectify and develop it. There are people who prefer ten-cent detective stories to Dickens and Hugo. There are others who would rather hear a jazz band than a great orchestra. And there are still others who dearly love to sing waltzes, ragtime and jingles in church. A real judge of devotional poetry can determine in a flash the relative merit of "Sweeter as the days go by" and "O Love that wilt not let me

[16] Pratt, *op. cit.*, pp. 69-71, suggests still another test, namely, the power of the hymn in actual use to impress "indifferent, immature, or half-participating users," and justly insists that "we surely have no right to allow the conception of Christianity to be lowered in such minds by trivial, perverted or misleading presentations of it."

go"; of "Grace, enough for me" [17] and "When I survey the wondrous cross".

The difference between the music of a good song and a trashy one is more easily apprehended than is the poetical discrepancy. Anybody with the slightest knowledge or appreciation of music can tell at once that "Count your blessings" is very, very bad, while "Love divine, all loves excelling" is superb; that "There is a green hill far away" is immeasurably superior to "He died for me" (although the latter is as close an imitation of the former, music, time and idea, as it can possibly be); that "Love is the theme" and "The King of Love my Shepherd is" are not to be mentioned in the same breath; that "Where we'll never grow old" is tawdry and "Hark! Hark! my soul" is sublime.

With the treasures of great souls available to us all, in our hymns, why must so many of us tie our spirits down to the poor, cheap twitterings of little money-chasing men and women? Why must we crawl along the ground and scour the street and the dance hall for the means of praise and thanksgiving, when we can scale Pisgah's lofty height and hold reverent communion with our Maker? Let us cast

[17] The second verse of this jewel runs as follows (italics, mine): "While standing there, my *trembling heart,* Once full of agony, could scarce believe the sight *I saw* Of grace, enough for me."

aside our careless, indifferent attitude, and thought-
fully, earnestly, prayerfully, strive to approach the
Throne with offerings of the best we can bring,—
to worship the Father in spirit and in truth!

CHAPTER III

MUSIC IN THE CHURCH AND SUNDAY SCHOOL

IN some sections of our country there is a sincere
effort being made to fight the cheaper sort of popular (secular) songs. Thoughtful men and women
are beginning to realize that many of the productions
of Tin Pan Alley are not only disgusting from the
point of view of music, but positively immoral in their
words. It is pleasant to be able to chronicle the fact
that wherever the attention of young people has
been sharply called to the real quality of the stuff
they have been singing, a great awakening and improvement have immediately ensued. For example,
one of our daily papers not long ago reprinted an
article from the *New York Evening Post*, describing
how the city of Madison, Wisconsin, promoted a campaign to teach the masses good music. Newspapers,
schools, stores, restaurants, moving picture theatres,
and churches assisted in pushing this campaign,
which was conceived and organized by the School
of Music of the University of Wisconsin. The theory
of this anti-jazz drive was as follows (as stated by
one of the University professors): "With their ears

filled with some of these hauntingly beautiful, simple melodies it will be more difficult for people to listen to the vulgar monotony of bad music. One selection a day was all that we presented to the public, and on that selection was concentrated most of our attention for that day. The selections ranged anywhere from 'Ol' Black Joe' to 'Moment Musicale'. I believe that the reason why many people think they do not like good music is that they are ignorant of it. It was to combat this condition that we started on our campaign. We wanted the people in general to see, what many of us are already fortunate enough to know, that good music does not necessarily mean heavy music or dull music".

The Literary Digest of Aug. 14, 1920, published some opinions upon the possibility of stamping out the more objectionable popular songs. War has been declared upon them, it appears, by the General Federation of Women's Clubs. One of the leaders in this fight recently wrote as follows: "I have worked for twenty years on the theory that jazz and ragtime, in its original form, would be the basis of the future American school [of composition]. But that is no reason why I can not see that ragtime and jazz, when vulgarized, are an actual menace to the life, morals, and education of young America to-day.

"When one knows that in one of Chicago's big-

gest and best high schools the students bought two
thousand popular songs in two weeks, and that the
committee of students appointed by the school found
only forty which they considered fit for boys and
girls to sing together, don't you really think something should happen to awaken American parents
to their responsibilities?

"In a Middle-Western city where I had been giving talks in which I attacked the evil popular songs
I said to the manager of a music-shop that I hoped
I had not hurt her business. She replied, 'If I could
help you in this campaign I'd give up everything
else in the world to do it'. She told me that seventy-
five per cent. of her customers were high-school boys
and girls who bought nothing but this trash, and
she said that they blushed when they asked for it."

Even the National Association of Masters of
Dancing is girding up its toes for the fray. If a
news item from New York City, under date of Aug.
27, 1920, may be credited, the Association, on the
preceding evening, listened with approval to a speak-
er who declared that the public had had too much
jazz and was turning toward more "natural" music.
He urged "a rigid censorship of words in music and
said suggestive lyrics should be discontinued". The
Association evolved a new step, described as slow
and graceful, called "The Wesleyan", "with the

avowed hope that it will receive approval of the Methodist Church, the anti-dancing edict of which the convention has deplored each day"!

Now, a fight against trash, in the field of secular or sacred song, is a difficult, discouraging, and almost endless affair. But a beginning has been made by many men and women, and there are thousands of people who only need to have their attention directed to the sort of stuff their children sing in the parlor and in the church to rise up in arms and swell the forces of decency everywhere.

In the preceding chapter the qualities and characteristics of cheap "religious" songs were set forth, together with their method of construction and the motives that actuate their authors and publishers. We must now consider how best to fight against their introduction into our churches, Sunday schools and young people's societies, and how most successfully to drive them out of the strongholds they have already occupied.

These tasks, as has been suggested, are of great difficulty, for two reasons. First, the love of cheap music has become, during the past ten or fifteen years, almost second nature to great masses of our people. They have acquired the habit of proclaiming loudly, and (strange to say) somewhat loftily, their ignorance of "classical" music, and of displaying clearly their supreme boredom when a courageous musician attempts to render some of it. We have all heard remarks like the following, delivered with a rather exasperating air of independence and superiority: "Well, I suppose that selection was very fine, but it was beyond *me; I* have never been trained in music, you see". As a matter of fact, numerous musical masterpieces *are* beyond the comprehension of the layman; but, on the other hand, just as many can be heard and thoroughly appreciated by persons with no training in music whatever. In other words, the trouble with the average listener is not inability to enjoy, but disinclination, usually based upon a wholly incorrect idea of what good music really is.

To fight against a state of mind is a task difficult enough, surely; but there is yet another consideration which at least doubles the difficulty. The writers and publishers of cheap songs might have given useful pointers on the dissemination of propaganda to the wretched crew at Potsdam before and during the Great War. The unworthy and frequently disreputable means they employ to advertise their wares have already been discussed. These men are of course thoroughly cognizant of the popular fondness for trash, and they are capitalizing it in a most efficient and disgraceful manner—disgraceful, because their millions are made through the degradation of the worship of God. Here, then, is the foe: a sort of two-headed beast, spitting out coruscating ragtime and jingles and poisonous onesteps and foxtrots, and creeping on his slimy belly into the very Holy of Holies.

The principle enunciated above (pp. 85-86) may be repeated here and insisted upon as fundamental, namely, that there can be no compromise whatsoever in this fight. If an accurate accounting could be taken of the profits which publishers of cheap hymn books make every year, at least half of such profits would probably be found to accrue from the Sunday school compromise, that is, from the sale of cheap books for Sunday school use only. He who compromises with a scorpion or a rattlesnake is lost; he who dallies with and coddles the equally poisonous dance hall hymn will soon be in full retreat, with the triumphant jeers of the publisher speeding him on his way.

To those pastors, superintendents, and choirmasters who have not yet surrendered their service of worship to Mammon I beg to submit the foregoing paragraph as containing full armor for the fray. For the cheap "hymn" almost invariably creeps into the church by way of the Sunday school; and if that entrance be closed fast and sure, in spite of the frantic appeals of the young people for "popular" songs, then the worship of God will be safe from contamination and pollution.

The task of *driving* out cheap books is far more

complicated and difficult than that of *keeping* them out. In order to accomplish the former successfully·and permanently, there must, first of all, be a deep and unalterable conviction in the minds of the minister and his co-workers of the vital importance of genuinely spiritual worship in all the various services which are held in the church or under its auspices. If there is any uncertainty or hesitation here, the task is absolutely hopeless.

In the second place, these leaders of the people must be equally deeply and unalterably convinced of the inherent cheapness and sorriness of the ragtime "hymn", and, therefore, of its absolute unfitness as a vehicle for prayer and praise. With these convictions as sword and shield, the fight may be begun hopefully and confidently. Without them— "God has the right to be worshipped with the best we have or can secure, even if the process of getting and bringing it costs us something. Indeed, if it costs nothing it means nothing. Every item of worship is an offering of joy and devotion to Him, and its worthiness is to be measured by what it means to the offerer. In too many prayer-meetings and other church services the devotional dignity of hymn-singing has been destroyed on this side. A poor book is used, which the people know to be poor and in their heart despise, because they are too mean to get a better one. Poor selections are kept in use, against which the feeling of the users more or less revolts, because they are too lazy and indifferent to attempt better ones. The leaders, both the minister and his musical helpers, have fallen into a disconsolate apathy about the exercise, and let it drag along in a stupid, poverty-stricken, listless fashion, not because they are without a sense of its manifest inferiority, but because they are averse to the effort to make it better. It will be noticed that it is not said that all churches should use the same books or the same hymns and tunes or the same general methods, for all churches are not alike. But the use by any church of that which it knows to be unworthy of itself and of God is so shameful that it is almost blasphemous. Counterfeit coin on the contribution-plate, vacant lip-service in the prayers, and doggerel and trash in the hymnody are pretty much alike as tributes of worship".[1]

Fortified, then, with these convictions, the minister, the superintendent, and the choirmaster must next set about implanting them firmly in the minds and hearts of the people. There are many ways in which this can be accomplished. The minister should, of course, begin the fight by some straight, earnest, fearless remarks from the pulpit. He will find many in the congregation to disagree with and criticise

[1] Pratt, *op. cit.,* pp. 64-65.

him, but let him hold his ground unflinchingly, staunch and steadfast in the knowledge that he is right. The superintendent, following the example of his chief, must explain to the Sunday school the violation of the proprieties involved in the singing of waltzes and onesteps in the house of God, and must make it clear even to the youngest that a commercialized hymnody has no place in true worship. The organist or choirmaster can be of inestimable value to both pastor and superintendent, for, as has been shown above, there is no better way of displaying the sorriness of a sorry "hymn" than by contrasting it, at the piano or organ, with a fine hymn. Only one copy of the cheap book needs to be saved from the bonfire for this purpose. Some such process of precept and example must be repeated over and over, for the development of good taste is a slow and tedious undertaking.

A song service on Sunday evening every month or so is an excellent means of presenting the best in hymnody to a congregation just stepping out of jazzdom. I do not mean a service in which the organist and the choir do most of the work, but one devoted almost exclusively to the singing of hymns, —to the widening of the congregational repertoire. Nearly all the great hymns have some incidents associated with their composition and use.[2] Let the

[2] *Cf.* footnote 5, p. 65.

minister relate these incidents, call attention to the thought around which the hymn is written and to its musical and lyric beauty, urge the people to fix their attention strongly on words and music, as they sing. The superintendent may use the same means in the Sunday school. He and the pastor will soon discover a genuine interest in hymns spreading through the congregation,—an interest that should be fostered and nourished by studies in hymnology at the mid-week prayer meeting or in the young people's societies.

Now, this program demands the outlay of a little money for the purchase of some six or eight books,[3] the giving of considerable time and labor to study, and the undiscouraged display of infinite patience in dealing with a jazz-loving congregation and Sunday school. But to drive out of God's house the unworthy and unholy songs that defile His worship, and to drive out of the hearts of the people the taste for them, is surely worth far more than even the most zealous of us ever will or can expend.

Nothing can take the place of congregational singing in the worship of God. And yet, in far too many churches, it is rather a dismal and uninspiring business. In the Preface and again in the second

---

[3] Consult the bibliography given on pages 201-213 of Professor Pratt's book (see footnote 20, p. 36).

chapter [4] of this little book, some suggestions were made as to the reasons for this most unfortunate condition. Where it exists, its immediate alteration is, barring the saving of souls, the most vital task that can possibly confront the minister and his assistants in the work of the Kingdom. For there can be no doubt that the deep spiritual enthusiasm aroused by hearty congregational singing tends to flow into all the various lines of church activity; and, conversely, that a lack of interest and of whole-souled participation in song exercises a dampening and repressing effect, not only upon the entire service but upon all good works.

Here, again, the minister must bestir himself to vigorous leadership, and must not allow discouragement on account of a possible absence of immediate results to drag him back to his former apathy. Stimulating, inspiring and helpful words from the pulpit, if often enough repeated, will gradually have their effect upon even the most indifferent congregation. But the burden falls equally upon the organist. A slipshod, inaccurate, blundering performer can never lead the people to new heights in song. And it may as well be said here that the chief function of an organist is to do just that thing. It makes no difference how gifted he may be at improvisation,

[4] P. 77.

how fine an ear he may have for combinations of
stops, how brilliantly he may execute preludes and
postludes. If he is unable to play hymns correctly,
vigorously, and inspiringly, he is *not* a church organist, and the sooner he resigns, the better. Perhaps one-tenth of the miserable dragging one hears
in so many churches is due to the inherent laziness
of human nature; a piddling, careless organist is
responsible for the other nine-tenths. Incidentally,
it is astounding how many young ladies who have
graduated in music at reputable colleges and con-
servatories are terror-stricken and helpless before a
simple hymn.

Some churches have a leader who stands out in a
prominent place and keeps the people from going
to sleep over their singing either by the sheer power
of his voice or by sundry gyrations and gesticula-
tions after the fashion of certain orchestra directors.
Such a performer is wholly superfluous in churches
which have pipe organs and genuine organists. For
assemblies, Sunday schools, and the like, he is almost
a necessity, though all too often he succeeds in making himself a colossal nuisance by his antediluvian
jokes and vulgar antics.

Good congregational singing is greatly stimulated
by wide-awake, energetic work in the choir gallery.
The chief function of the choir, as of the organist, is
to lead the people in the hymns. In some of our

city churches the choir occupies, queerly enough, a loft at the end of the church opposite the pulpit, and so sings at the backs of the people in the pews, instead of into their faces. But that situation is comparatively unusual, for the large majority of choirs are conspicuously seated near the minister, where they can actually lead in the service of song.

Sunday school orchestras are much favored in some cities, and they may possibly be valuable; but my observation is that where orchestras are found, there trashy music is found, also. Cheap books are "orchestrated" (as a further inducement, of course, to their purchase), and when five or six young people get their violins, cornets and trombones going full tilt on some wretched piece of "sacred" jazz, it is quite easy to close your eyes and imagine yourself in a dance hall. A good pianist and a leader with a deep sense of the proprieties of a religious service are far better.

Hearty congregational singing is always stimulated by a judicious selection of hymns. Most people come to church reverently and worshipfully, and so are better prepared to sing vigorously a song of praise at the opening of the service, such as "Ye servants of God, your Master proclaim", than some mournful dirge like "I'm but a stranger here". Similarly, the selections following the scripture and the sermon should be germane and pertinent.

So, by wise selection and inspiring leadership, in which minister, superintendent, organist, and choir must all share, the service of song may be made, in every church and Sunday school in the land, a worthy offering of sweet savor unto the Lord.

Before leaving the subject of congregational singing, one more word must be added by way of emphasis. If the minister hesitates or falters, the whole program might as well take the place of the trash books on the bonfire. It is quite true, of course, that many seminaries offer practically no instruction in hymnology (a most unfortunate and inexplicable state of affairs), and that in many Bible schools and institutes Mr. Jazz and Mr. Gotrox have charge of the department of "Gospel Song". In spite of this, however, no minister has any excuse to plead ignorance, for a little study will open up to him one of the most fascinating fields in the whole realm of religious thought and achievement. If he pleads indifference, he needs to have his eyes opened to the paramount importance of vigorous singing, and to his duty of energetic leadership in it; and if he will not submit to the process of a charging of his hymnodic batteries, let him, for the good of the church and the glory of God, move on and give place to some more enlightened and energetic man who is *not* indifferent to the transcendent significance of genuine worship.

Every one of the great denominations has one or

more hymnals of the highest quality. The names and publishers of these books can be easily ascertained by inquiry, and their merits tested by careful examination. It is exceedingly important that there should be an ample supply of books, with words *and* music, so that everybody who desires to take part in the service of song may do so without the inconvenience of being compelled either to look over shoulders and around hats or to sing from memory.

We must now return to the choir and the organist and consider the question of "special music". One or two general observations may first be made. Many choirs have an inexcusably bad habit of chatting in the choir gallery after they have taken their places for the service. This practice has an exceedingly injurious effect upon the people in the pews, who, perceiving that their leaders are totally oblivious of the proprieties of the sanctuary, follow with great complacency the example so prominently set. The result is that when the minister steps into the pulpit, he faces a sort of general social party, with numerous groups twittering away in a most affable and pleasant manner, instead of a reverent assemblage of worshipers, with their hearts open to the inspiration of the hour. Incidentally, the organist's prelude, which should be a sort of devotional introduction to the whole service, might just as well be rendered in the heart of Africa, for most of the people are amiably gossiping, and those who really want to hear the music must be satisfied to listen instead to certain harrowing details about somebody's new dress or to an animated discussion of crops or business prospects.

Part of the blame for the existence of such a sacrilegious atmosphere is certainly to be placed on the minister. Now, I am not a member of a ritualistic church, but my observation has been that in such churches there is invariably a genuine reverence for the place and the service. The minister who without an ordered liturgy makes his own program of worship, and carries it out according to his own ideas, must see to it as best he can that a tradition of respect for the sanctuary is developed in the hearts of his people, too. The slipshod informality and general uncertainty (with its consequent embarrassment) so frequently to be seen in non-liturgical services is inexcusable, for it stimulates irreverence and a wandering of the attention entirely incompatible with that worshipful concentration of soul so essential to the success of any religious assemblage. I am not pleading for the universal adoption of liturgies, but for a carefully arranged program, carried out with dignity and a decent regard for the proprieties of the Lord's house.

At the risk of being accused of desertion of non-ritualistic precedent, I desire to register here my conviction that the choir, or at least the women members of it, should wear some sort of robe. The weekly display of variegated millinery and more or less brilliant gowns and suits in the choir loft is too much like a fashion show to escape general observation and comment from the feminine (and some of the masculine) portion of the audience. When the hymns are sung, some awe-inspiring hat or dazzling dress is sure to distract attention from the act of worship then in progress; whereas, if the men and women in the choir wore black robes (the women, caps, also), the fashion show would give place to a body of Christians unostentatiously striving to promote the worship of God.

Some denominational leaders have made up their minds that anthems, solos, etc., are wholly out of place in church. These men lose no opportunity of casting slurs at "special music which is over the heads of the people," and of hinting quite strongly that the time occupied in its rendition is worse than wasted. This sort of criticism is justified only when the organist and his singers abandon the devotional for the concert style of anthems and other musical numbers; and that happens very infrequently in well-regulated choirs. There is no danger that music will ever be over-emphasized in the great majority of our churches. On the contrary, in many of them religion seeks very little aid and inspiration from

that fine art which is really the child of the Church [5]
and which has contributed so bounteously and so
beautifully to the bringing in of the Kingdom during the past centuries.

Every remark that has been made in this book
concerning good and bad hymns applies equally
to good and bad anthems. For the anthem is
also an act of worship, or it has no right to be
performed in church. There are a large number
of writers and publishers of cheap anthems, and
they are just as happy and busy as their blood-
brothers of the song book industry. The cheap anthem is usually to be distinguished by the difficult
and dangerous feats it requires of all the singers,
but more particularly of the bassos. A choir that
sings trash of this sort ought always to have an
ambulance ready to cart bassos to the hospital when
they collapse after the awful Sunday morning strain
of ripping and tearing up and down the scale. Not
only the cheap anthem is to be shunned, but also
the florid, concertistic anthem, which, however skill-
fully composed, is out of place in the devotional
atmosphere of the sanctuary. It hardly needs to
be added that a sensible choirmaster will gauge
accurately the musical ability of his singers and
will never, under any circumstances, have them sing

[5] Read Pratt's excellent chapter on "Religion and the Art of
Music," *op. cit.,* pp. 9–44.

compositions which are beyond the range of their powers. It is far, far better to render some beautiful and appropriate hymn as the offertory, than to murder Sullivan's magnificent "Sing, O Heavens," or the incomparable "Hallelujah Chorus."

There are ample treasures of good anthems for choirs of every grade of ability.[6] And no fairminded person can dispute the effectiveness, *as an act of worship*, of a devotional anthem, selected for its bearing on the scripture and the sermon of the hour, and sung by the choir with reverence and genuine spiritual insight.

That leads me to say that the members of volunteer choirs should certainly be Christian men and women, whom the congregation can follow in worship without any reservation whatever. In the case of paid musicians, this rule, unfortunately, can not always be observed.

The chorus choir seems to me much better, from every point of view, than the quartet. It is, of course, vastly more efficient in the leadership of congregational singing, which is, as has already been said, the principal business of choirs. And in the rendering of anthems, a full body of tone is actually more effective than the artistic shading in which the quartet excels. Besides, membership in the choir

[6] Consult Randall's "Choirmaster's Guide to Hymns and Anthems," Novello, London, 1911; or Foster's "Anthems and Anthem Composers," Novello, London, 1901.

means real Christian service; and men and women of musical ability should be given this opportunity of using their talents for the glory of God.

Organ and vocal solos should be selected with care, upon the same principle that governs the choice of anthems. In short, every piece of music played or sung in the house of the Lord should be regarded as an act of worship, and should be chosen and rendered with absolutely no other object than of making a real contribution to the inspiration and the spiritual power of the service.

The volunteer choir has, sad to say, become rather famous for petty squabbles, started over nothing, and sometimes fanned into great, roaring feuds that have even been known to split churches. No man or woman ought ever to become a member of a choir who does not possess enough of the spirit of toleration and of real Christian love to make such disastrous occurrences impossible.

Choir work, if well done, demands genuine consecration, and not a little time, energy and self-sacrifice. In consideration of that fact, there should be, in the congregation, a spirit of hearty coöperation with the singers, of gratitude for their services, of interest in their work; with never a word of bitterness or ugly sarcasm, no matter how inexpertly they may render the anthem. They are very probably doing the best they can,—and, what is more important,—if they are sincere Christians, they are doing it for the glory of God.

There could be no more appropriate way to close this little book than to repeat the words which stand on the title-page, for they express concisely and completely the point of view these chapters have tried to present: "Let the word of Christ dwell in you richly in all wisdom; teaching and admonishing one another in psalms and hymns and spiritual songs, singing with grace in your hearts to the Lord."

APPENDIX

A charge to keep I have
A parting hymn we sing
A voice is heard on earth
Abide with me
Alas! and did my Savior bleed
All for Jesus—All for Jesus
All glory, laud and honor
All hail the power of Jesus' name
All my heart this night rejoices
All praise to Thee, my God, this night
Alleluia! Song of gladness
Am I a soldier of the cross
Ancient of days, Who sittest
Angels from the realms of glory
Angel voices ever singing

[1] This list is not given as a canon of sacred song, but simply
to serve as a practical guide in the actual selection of hymns.
It is very small, of necessity, but the hymns in it may be sung
at any religious meeting, by old people or young people, and
not only be sung, but understood and appreciated. It includes
a few selections for a variety of topics and times, and also
some of the best "Gospel Hymns." Practically every hymn
in this list will be found in any standard hymnal.

Another year is dawning
Approach, my soul, the mercy-seat
Arm of the Lord, awake
Arm these Thy soldiers, mighty Lord
Around the throne of God in heaven
Around Thy grave, Lord Jesus
Art thou weary, art thou languid
As with gladness men of old
Asleep in Jesus
At even, ere the sun was set
Awake my soul, in joyful lays (Park Street)
Awake, my soul, stretch every nerve
Away in a manger

Before Jehovah's awful throne
Begin, my tongue, some heavenly theme (Manoah)
Behold a Stranger at the door
Beneath the cross of Jesus
Blessed are the sons of God
Blest be the tie that binds
Bread of the world, in mercy broken
Break Thou the bread of life
Brightest and best of the sons of the morning
Brightly gleams our banner

Christ is made the sure foundation
Christ is risen, Christ is risen
Christ the Lord is risen to-day

Come, Holy Spirit, Dove divine
Come, Holy Spirit, heavenly Dove
Come, let us join our cheerful songs
Come, let us join with faithful souls
Come, my soul, thou must be waking
Come, Thou Almighty King
Come unto me; it is the Savior's voice
Come unto Me, ye weary
Come, we that love the Lord (St. Thomas)
Come, ye disconsolate
Come, ye faithful, raise the strain
Come, ye thankful people, come
Consider the lilies, how stately they grow
Courage, brother! do not stumble
Cross of Jesus, cross of sorrow
Crown Him with many crowns

Day is dying in the West
Dear Lord and Father of mankind
Depth of mercy, can there be

Encamped along the hills of light
Eternal Light! eternal Light!

Fairest Lord Jesus
Faith of our fathers
Father, again in Jesus' name we meet
Father, whate'er of earthly bliss

Fight the good fight with all thy might
Fling out the banner
For all thy saints who from their labors rest
For the beauty of the earth
From all Thy saints in warfare
From every stormy wind that blows
From Greenland's icy mountains

Glorious things of thee are spoken
Glory and praise and honor
Go, labor on, spend and be spent
Go to dark Gethsemane
God be with you, till we meet again
God, in the gospel of His Son
God is love, by Him upholden
God is love; His mercy brightens
God is the refuge of His saints
God moves in a mysterious way (Dundee)
God of our fathers, Whose almighty hand
God's trumpet wakes the slumbering world
God, that madest earth and heaven
Golden harps are sounding
Guide me, O Thou great Jehovah

Hail to the brightness of Zion's glad morning
Hark! Hark! my soul
Hark! my soul, it is the Lord
Hark! ten thousand harps and voices

Hark! the herald angels sing
Hark! the sound of holy voices
Hark! what mean these holy voices
He leadeth me: O blessed thought
He that goeth forth with weeping
High in the heavens, eternal God
Holy Ghost, with light divine
Holy, Holy, Holy
Holy night, peaceful night
Hosanna! loud hosanna!
How firm a foundation
How gentle God's commands
How sweet the name of Jesus sounds

I am thine, O Lord
I gave my life for thee
I hear the Savior say
I hear Thy welcome voice
I know my heavenly Father knows
I know that my Redeemer lives
I lay my sins on Jesus
I love Thy Kingdom, Lord (St. Thomas)
I love to tell the story
I need Thee every hour
I think when I read that sweet story
If through unruffled seas
Immortal Love, forever full
In the cross of Christ I glory

In the hour of trial
In the secret of His presence
It came upon the midnight clear
I've found a friend; O such a friend

Jesus, and shall it ever be
Jesus calls us; o'er the tumult
Jesus, I my cross have taken (Autumn)
Jesus, keep me near the cross
Jesus, lover of my soul
Jesus, Savior, pilot me
Jesus shall reign where'er the sun
Jesus, the very thought of Thee
Jerusalem, the golden (Ewing)
Joy to the world, the Lord is come
Just as I am, without one plea

Lead, kindly Light
Lead us, O Father, in the paths of peace
Lo! He comes, with clouds descending
Look, ye saints, the sight is glorious (Coronae)
Lord, dismiss us with Thy blessing
Lord, for tomorrow and its needs
Lord Jesus, I long to be perfectly whole
Lord of our life, and God of our salvation
Lord, speak to me, that I may speak
Lord, with glowing heart I'd praise Thee
Love divine, all loves excelling
Low in the grave He lay

Majestic sweetness sits enthroned
Mighty God, while angels bless Thee
Mine eyes have seen the glory
More love to Thee, O Christ
Must Jesus bear the cross alone
My country, 'tis of thee
My days are gliding swiftly by
My faith looks up to Thee
My God, and Father, while I stray
My God, I thank Thee, Who hast made
My hope is built on nothing less
My Jesus, as Thou wilt
My Jesus, I love Thee, I know Thou art mine
My soul, be on thy guard

Nearer, my God, to Thee
New every morning is the love
No shadows yonder
Not half has ever been told
Not worthy, Lord, to gather up the crumbs
Now God be with us, for the night is closing
Now the day is over

O beautiful for spacious skies
O come, all ye faithful
O could I speak the matchless worth
O day of rest and gladness
O for a closer walk with God

O for a heart to praise my God
O God, beneath Thy guiding hand
O God, our help in ages past
O God, the Rock of Ages
O happy band of pilgrims
O happy day, that fixed my choice
O holy Father, strong to save
O holy Savior! Friend unseen
O Jesus, I have promised
O Jesus, Thou art standing
O Jesus, when I think of Thee
O Lamb of God! still keep me
O little town of Bethlehem
O Love that wilt not let me go (St. Margaret)
O Master, let me walk with Thee
O Mother dear, Jerusalem
O Paradise! O Paradise!
O perfect Love, all human thought transcending
O safe to the Rock that is higher than I
O say, can you see
O Word of God incarnate
O worship the King, all glorious above
O Zion, haste
On our way rejoicing
On the mountain top appearing (Zion)
Once in royal David's city
One sweetly solemn thought
Onward, Christian soldiers

Our blest Redeemer, ere He breathed
Our Lord is risen from the dead
Out of my bondage, sorrow and night

Pass me not, O gentle Savior
Peace, perfect peace
Pleasant are Thy courts above
Praise God, from whom all blessings flow
Praise, my soul, the King of heaven
Praise the Lord, ye heavens adore Him
Praise ye the Father, for His loving-kindness
Purer yet and purer

Rejoice, all ye believers
Rejoice, ye pure in heart
Rise, my soul, and stretch thy wings
Rock of Ages
Round the Lord in glory seated

Safe in the arms of Jesus
Safely through another week
Saints of God, the dawn is brightening
Savior, again to Thy dear name we raise
Savior, breathe an evening blessing
Savior, like a shepherd lead us
Savior, Thy dying love
Savior, when in dust to Thee
Shall we gather at the river

Sleep on, beloved
Sleep thy last sleep
So let our lips and lives express
Softly now the light of day
Soldiers of Christ, arise
Songs of praise the angels sang
Spirit of God, descend upon my heart
Stand up, stand up for Jesus
Still, still with Thee
Sun of my soul, Thou Savior dear
Sweet hour of prayer
Sweet is the work, my God, my King

Take my life and let it be
Tell me the old, old story
Ten thousand times ten thousand
The Church's one foundation
The corn is ripe for reaping
The day is gently sinking to a close
The day is past and over
The day of resurrection
The first Noël
The Homeland! O the Homeland!
The King of Love my Shepherd is
The Lord be with us as we bend
The Lord is my Shepherd
The morning light is breaking
The ninety and nine

The radiant morn hath passed away
The roseate hues of early dawn
The sands of time are sinking
The shadows of the evening hour
The Son of God goes forth to war
The spacious firmament on high
The strife is o'er, the battle done
The voice that breathed o'er Eden
There is a fountain filled with blood (Cowper)
There is a green hill far away
There is an hour of peaceful rest
There is no name so sweet on earth
There's a friend for little children
There's a Stranger at the door
There's a wideness in God's mercy
This rite our blest Redeemer gave
Thou art my Shepherd
Thou didst leave Thy throne
Thou, Whose almighty word
To Thee, my God and Savior

Upward where the stars are burning

Watchman, tell us of the night
We are living, we are dwelling
We have heard the joyful sound
We march, we march to victory
We may not climb the heavenly steeps

We three Kings of Orient are
We would see Jesus
Weary of earth and laden with my sin
Welcome, delightful morn
Welcome, happy morning! age to age shall say
What a Friend we have in Jesus
When all Thy mercies, O my God
When He cometh, when He cometh
When, His salvation bringing
When I survey the wondrous cross
When morning gilds the skies
When peace like a river
When thy heart, with joy o'erflowing
Where cross the crowded ways of life
While shepherds watched their flocks by night
While with ceaseless course the sun
Who is on the Lord's side
With gladsome hearts we come
With happy voices singing
Work, for the night is coming

Ye Christian heralds, go proclaim
Ye servants of God, your Master proclaim

INDEX